Survival Vocabulary Stories

Learning Words in Context

Katherine
Whitten

WALCH PUBLISHING®

User's Guide
to
Walch Reproducible Books

As part of our general effort to provide educational materials which are as practical and economical as possible, we have designated this publication a "reproducible book." The designation means that purchase of the book includes purchase of the right to limited reproduction of all pages on which this symbol appears:

Here is the basic Walch policy: We grant to individual purchasers of this book the right to make sufficient copies of reproducible pages for use by all students of a single teacher. This permission is limited to a single teacher, and does not apply to entire schools or school systems, so institutions purchasing the book should pass the permission on to a single teacher. Copying of the book or its parts for resale is prohibited.

Any questions regarding this policy or requests to purchase further reproduction rights should be addressed to:

Permissions Editor
J. Weston Walch, Publisher
P. O. Box 658
Portland, Maine 04104-0658

SUSTAINABLE FORESTRY INITIATIVE

Certified Chain of Custody
Promoting Sustainable Forest Management
www.sfiprogram.org

SGS-SFI/COC-US09/5501

1   2   3   4   5   6   7   8   9   10

ISBN 0-8251-2863-3

This collection of stories is dedicated to my family, whose help, ideas, and advice have been invaluable. My children, Todd and Sarah, deserve special thanks for their patience and willingness to be "readers." I would also like to acknowledge Bette Chamberlain and Dan-Ling Fu for their steadfast support.

Contents

To the Teacher

The goal of this publication is to improve reading comprehension skills through stories that teach a core of basic vocabulary and present real-life situations with which students can identify. Questions following the stories label which comprehension skill is being tapped. They appear in order of increasing difficulty, from literal recall to inferential thinking. After a student has completed a few stories and the accompanying skill work, you will be able to identify the areas of reading comprehension that are strengths and weaknesses of the student. You may wish to develop additional activities to try to strengthen the weak areas.

The stories in this collection are designed for use with students in grades six through twelve whose reading levels are between grades two and six. The majority of the stories are written at the grade three level, based on the Fry Readability Scale. The exact reading level for each story is indicated in parentheses in the table of contents. Twenty vocabulary words form the core vocabulary for the five stories in each unit, though not all twenty words are necessarily used in each story within a unit. These vocabulary words are taught in the J. Weston Walch publication *Survival Vocabulary*, written by Gertrude Wedler. *Survival Vocabulary Stories* is intended to provide the opportunity for students to extend their knowledge of new vocabulary to the reading process.

Although these stories may be used effectively as a follow-up to *Survival Vocabulary*, it is not necessary for students to have prior exposure to that publication. You may need to pre-teach the vocabulary to students who have not already studied it. Some students may need special emphasis on the decoding of the twenty words, but may have no trouble with understanding the meaning of the words. Students for whom English is a second language may need instruction in both decoding and comprehension of the vocabulary.

The vocabulary lists, the stories, and the exercises are reproducible. You can make as many copies of the pages as you need for the students in your classes.

Before reading the stories, students will benefit by reading the words several times, studying the meanings of the words, and discussing the meanings with their peers. You may wish to create some vocabulary activities such as matching the word and the definition, matching the word to an appropriate picture, or having the students use the words in oral or written sentences. As they read a story, or after they have read one, students could underline the key vocabulary words each time they occur in the story.

Often I have suggested a writing activity at the end of a story; and I believe students will improve both their retention of the vocabulary and their comprehension skills if they write frequently, using the vocabulary presented in the unit. You can also extend the study of the unit through class discussion of some of the topics presented or through students' oral sharing of their written work. For the students who have trouble with language arts skills, an integrated approach to reading, writing, thinking, and speaking will provide a rich environment for improvement.

Vocabulary Words and Definitions

Unit 1. Home Words

1. **apartment**   a room or set of rooms in a house or building, for people to live in

2. **house**   a building for living in

3. **kitchen**   a room where cooking is done

4. **bedroom**   a room to sleep in

5. **bathroom**   a room in which to take a bath or shower and use the toilet

6. **living room**   a sitting room for family use

7. **cable**   a TV connection that offers a clear picture and extra programs

8. **video**   a tape of a movie, show, or event that is played on a TV set

9. **sink**   a basin with running water and a drain, found in the kitchen and bathroom

10. **toilet**   a bowl with a seat and drain and with a water tank to flush the bowl clean, found in the bathroom

11. **bathtub**   a large tub in which to wash the body

12. **stove**   an item for cooking and heating food

13. **refrigerator**   a large box for keeping food cold

14. **microwave**   an oven that heats and cooks food fast

15. **chair**   a seat with a back, for one person

16. **lamp**   an item that gives light

17. **couch**   a long seat having a back and arms

18. **closet**   a small room for hanging clothes and storing things

19. **rug**   a thick floor mat

20. **key**   a small tool used to lock and unlock; also, something that explains the symbols or markings used on a map or chart

Vocabulary Words and Definitions

Unit 2. Food Words

1.	**vegetables**	plants or parts of plants that may be eaten
2.	**fish**	the flesh of an underwater animal used for food
3.	**bread**	a baked food made mainly of flour
4.	**meat**	the flesh of animals used for food
5.	**milk**	a white liquid produced by female mammals to feed their babies; white liquid drawn from cows used by humans to drink and make dairy products
6.	**soup**	a liquid food made by boiling meat, vegetables, etc.
7.	**eggs**	hard-shelled oval objects laid by chickens and used for food
8.	**butter**	a yellow, fatty food made from cream
9.	**coffee**	a dark brown drink made from the beans of a coffee tree
10.	**soda**	a sweet, fizzy soft drink
11.	**tea**	a drink made by pouring boiling water over dried leaves
12.	**fruit**	part of a plant that has the seeds and may be eaten
13.	**sugar**	sweet, white powder or crystals made from sugarcane or sugar beets
14.	**breakfast**	the first meal of the day
15.	**lunch**	the second or noon meal
16.	**supper**	the last meal of the day
17.	**cookies**	small flat cakes
18.	**juice**	the liquid part of fruit, vegetables, and meat
19.	**snack**	small amount of food eaten between meals
20.	**cereal**	a food made of grain

Vocabulary Words and Definitions

Unit 3. Family Words

1. **mother**   a female parent

2. **father**   a male parent

3. **sister**   a woman or girl related to you by having the same parents

4. **brother**   a man or boy related to you by having the same parents

5. **guardian**   a person appointed to take care of another

6. **children**   young boys and girls; sons and daughters in a family

7. **aunt**   your father's or mother's sister; your uncle's wife

8. **uncle**   your father's or mother's brother; your aunt's husband

9. **niece**   your sister's or brother's daughter

10. **nephew**   your sister's or brother's son

11. **cousin**   the son or daughter of your uncle or aunt

12. **grandmother**   your father's or mother's mother

13. **grandfather**   your father's or mother's father

14. **parents**   a father and mother

15. **wife**   a woman to whom a man is married

16. **husband**   a man to whom a woman is married

17. **daughter**   a person's female child

18. **son**   a person's male child

19. **stepmother**   woman married to your father after the death or divorce of your mother

20. **stepfather**   man married to your mother after the death or divorce of your father

Vocabulary Words and Definitions

Unit 4. Time Words

1. **clock** — an item used for measuring time by means of pointers moving over a dial or by progressing numbers, usually not worn or carried by the user

2. **watch** — an item used for measuring time which is worn or carried by the user

3. **hands** — the pointers on a clock or watch

4. **digital** — time shown in numbers

5. **calendar** — a chart showing the days, weeks, and months of a year

6. **day** — a period of twenty-four hours, or the period of light between sunrise and sunset

7. **week** — a time unit of seven days

8. **month** — a time unit of four weeks or about thirty days

9. **year** — a time unit of twelve months

10. **hour** — a time unit of sixty minutes; twenty-four of these units make one day

11. **minute** — a time unit of sixty seconds; sixty of these units make one hour

12. **second** — the smallest time unit; sixty of these units make one minute

13. **A.M.** — before noon

14. **P.M.** — after noon

15. **morning** — the first part of the day, from dawn to noon

16. **noon** — the middle of the day at twelve o'clock

17. **afternoon** — the time from noon to evening

18. **evening** — the close of day, between afternoon and night

19. **night** — the period of time from sunset to sunrise

20. **date** — the time of an event; the day, month, and year when it happens

Vocabulary Words and Definitions

Unit 5. Food Store Words

1. **supermarket**   a large store selling food and other goods

2. **groceries**   food and household items

3. **cart**   a container used to carry groceries

4. **checkout**   a counter where groceries are paid for

5. **cashier**   the person at the checkout who is in charge of money

6. **coupon**   a printed slip of paper used to get a certain amount of money off the price of an item

7. **produce**   crops grown by a farmer and sold at the supermarket

8. **bakery**   a place where bread and pastries are sold

9. **department**   a section of a store

10. **frozen**   as cold and as hard as ice

11. **aisle**   a walkway between rows of stacked items

12. **manager**   the person in charge

13. **clerk**   a person who sells in a store

14. **food stamps**   pieces of paper issued to people for use as cash to buy food

15. **brown bag**   a paper holder in which to put groceries or other items

16. **enter**   to go in or come in

17. **exit**   a way out

18. **deli**   a place where prepared and cooked foods are sold

19. **receipt**   a slip of paper marked with the amount paid

20. **change**   money owed to a person who pays more than is due

Vocabulary Words and Definitions

Unit 6. School Words

1. **class**   a group of students being taught together

2. **teacher**   a person who shows how to do something or explains something

3. **period**   length of time for one class; also, a dot at the end of a sentence

4. **auditorium**   a large room where groups of people meet to listen to speeches or watch plays and concerts

5. **cafeteria**   a large dining area where people buy food and carry it to a table to eat

6. **fire drill**   practice leaving the building in case of fire

7. **computer**   a machine that processes and stores information

8. **desk**   a piece of furniture with a flat top on which to write

9. **pencil**   a pointed tool with lead in it with which to write

10. **paper**   a thin sheet used for writing, printing, or wrapping

11. **office**   a place where most of the paperwork is done for a school or a business

12. **principal**   the head person in a school

13. **Internet**   a huge computer network where information can be found and shared

14. **bell**   something that makes a ringing sound

15. **software**   the program or instructions that tell a computer what to do

16. **gym**   a large room for games and exercise; also, physical education class

17. **microchip**   a tiny square of thin material used in electronic equipment

18. **board**   a flat, dark surface used to write on with chalk; a group of people who advise or manage a school or company

19. **chalk**   soft white limestone used to write on dark chalkboards

20. **homework**   schoolwork done at home

Survival Vocabulary Stories

Vocabulary Words and Definitions

Unit 7. Health Words

1. **healthy** being well; a good condition of the body

2. **doctor** a person trained to treat people who are sick or hurt

3. **sick** having some disease or illness

4. **ache** a dull pain that lasts for a while

5. **hurt** to have pain

6. **sore** painful

7. **sprain** an injury to a joint in which the tendons or ligaments are stretched or twisted, but no bones are broken

8. **clinic** a place where sick people are treated and released

9. **hospital** a place where sick people are cared for and may stay overnight

10. **ambulance** an emergency vehicle for bringing sick or injured people to the hospital

11. **emergency** something serious that happens suddenly and calls for fast action

12. **vitamin** a substance needed for normal body growth and health

13. **antiseptic** something that kills germs

14. **bandage** a cover for a cut or other injury

15. **appointment** an arrangement to be somewhere at a certain time

16. **nurse** a person who takes care of the sick

17. **lab technician** a person who tests blood and other samples

18. **midwife** a person who helps women give birth

19. **dentist** a doctor whose work is caring for teeth

20. **medicine** something to help improve or cure a disease or illness

Vocabulary Words and Definitions

Unit 8. Community Words

1.	**factory**	a place where things are made
2.	**garage**	a building where cars are parked or repaired
3.	**laundry**	a place where clothes and linens are washed
4.	**pharmacy**	a store where medicine and other items are sold
5.	**sidewalk**	a place at the side of a street where people can walk
6.	**synagogue**	a building where Jews worship
7.	**church**	a building where Christians worship
8.	**police officer**	a person who keeps order or directs traffic
9.	**fire station**	a building for people and equipment that put out fires
10.	**post office**	a place where mail is handled and postage stamps are sold
11.	**mall**	a large building containing a variety of shops
12.	**mailbox**	a box from which mail is collected or to which mail is delivered
13.	**barber**	a person who cuts other people's hair
14.	**superintendent**	a person who oversees something or is in charge of an apartment building
15.	**plumber**	a person who installs and repairs pipes
16.	**restaurant**	a place to buy and eat a meal
17.	**theater**	a place where movies are shown or plays are acted
18.	**bank**	a place for saving, borrowing, or exchanging money
19.	**school**	a place for teaching and learning
20.	**library**	a place where many books are kept; a place which lends books to people

Vocabulary Words and Definitions

Unit 9. Restaurant Words

1. **booth** — a partly enclosed space with a table and seats for several people; a small room or enclosed compartment

2. **counter** — a long table

3. **menu** — a list of food served in a restaurant

4. **order** — a serving of food asked for in a restaurant

5. **napkin** — a folded cloth or paper used at meals for protecting clothing and for wiping lips or fingers

6. **ladies' room** — a bathroom for women and girls

7. **men's room** — a bathroom for men and boys

8. **pasta** — a dish of cooked macaroni, spaghetti, or such

9. **reservation** — an arrangement to have a table ready for a person

10. **appetizer** — food eaten before a meal to increase the desire for more food

11. **salad** — a dish of raw vegetables

12. **sandwich** — slices of bread with a filling between them

13. **dessert** — food eaten at the end of a meal

14. **takeout** — food removed from a restaurant and eaten somewhere else

15. **waitress** — a woman who serves food

16. **waiter** — a man who serves food

17. **table** — a piece of furniture having a flat top on legs

18. **espresso** — coffee brewed by forcing steam through ground roasted beans

19. **check** — a written statement of the amount owed in a restaurant

20. **entrance** — a place through which a person goes in or comes in

Vocabulary Words and Definitions

Unit 10. Travel Words

1. **bus** a large motor vehicle that can carry many people and usually follows a regular route

2. **train** a line of connected railroad cars on a track, pulled or pushed by a locomotive

3. **cab** a car for public use with a driver who is paid

4. **car** a four-wheeled vehicle driven on streets and roads

5. **airplane/jet** a machine with wings that carries people and flies through the air

6. **subway** an underground electric railway

7. **boat** a watercraft moved by oars, sails, or engine

8. **bicycle** a vehicle to ride on with two wheels, handle bars, a seat, and foot pedals to move it

9. **truck** a vehicle for hauling loads along the streets

10. **ticket** a small printed card that gives a person the right to travel somewhere on a public vehicle or to enter a place with an admission fee

11. **conductor** a person in charge of passengers who collects tickets or money

12. **driver** a person who makes a vehicle move

13. **walk** to move along on foot

14. **pilot** a person who flies an airplane or steers a boat

15. **elevator** a small, cage-like room that moves people up and down from floor to floor in tall buildings

16. **helmet** a protective covering for the head

17. **seat belt** a strap that holds a person in a seat

18. **fare** the amount of money paid for a ride

19. **motorcycle** a two-wheeled vehicle moved by an engine, larger and heavier than a bicycle

20. **map** a chart that shows roads, cities, and other surface features

Answers to Exercises

Unit 1. Home Words

Story 1

1. house
2. dark blue
3. livingroom
4. her list and pencil
5. they had a good time there
   (Answers will vary.)
6. Answers will vary.

Story 2

1. c
2. b
3. c
4. a
5. c
6. Answers will vary.

Story 3

Answers will vary.
1. This story is about what Sonya will have to do as an apartment cleaner.
2. In the kitchen, Sonya will have to clean the oven, refrigerator, stove top, microwave, and counters. She will also scrub the sink and empty the trash. She will wash the floor.
3. After she cleans the kitchen, she will clean the bathroom.
4. will not hire her
5. Answers will vary.
6. Answers will vary.

Story 4

1. Answers will vary.
2. a closet for brooms and mops and a place for the washer
3. Guy; basement apartment
4. Mrs. Morin is going to make him live downstairs in the apartment
5. it didn't take him long to draw the plans for the apartment in the basement.
   (Answers may vary.)
6. Answers will vary.

Story 5

1. a
2. c
3. a
4. a

5. Answers may vary. The second part of the answer should support the first part.
6. Answers will vary.

Unit 2. Food Words

Story 1

1. c
2. b
3. a

4. b
5. b

Story 2

1. boys trying to cook on a camping trip
2. egg sandwiches; juice and cookies
3. got onto the school bus
4. they were in the bottom of his pack under other things
5. he had never tried to cook pancakes before
6. Answers will vary.

Story 3

1. Answers may vary.
2. the food pyramid
3. they put pictures of food into different groups
4. Mr. Millo called on him to answer a question
5. he loves to eat
6. Answers will vary.

Story 4

1. b
2. c
3. a

4. c
5. b

Story 5

1. a boy from Cambodia, who isn't used to food in the United States
2. rice or soup
3. he tried to talk to him

4. he liked the meat better
5. he had a new friend to help him with new things

Unit 3. Family Words

Story 1

1. trip; family
2. red silk dress
3. about a big dinner
4. Lee's mother will know who she is
5. he would have someone to play with
6. c

Story 2

1. a
2. eighteen
3. a
4. c
5. b
6. Answers will vary.

Story 3

1. c
2. b
3. a
4. b
5. a
6. Answers will vary.

Story 4

1. tickets
2. only
3. twenty
4. Carl
5. he will have enough for his family
6. b

Story 5

1. c
2. b
3. a
4. c
5. c

Unit 4. Time Words

Story 1

1. b
2. c
3. a
4. a
5. b
6. Answers will vary.

Story 2

1. fell asleep in study hall on the first day of school
2. a computer game on it; run laps around the field
3. digital clock; alarm
4. he was not in very good shape
5. he thought it was morning

Story 3

1. Answers will vary.
2. carpenter's apron
3. June; a time one hundred years later
4. rock back and forth
5. she hears sounds like the sounds the robots made
6. Answers will vary.

Story 4

1. b
2. b
3. if there was a telephone; called the ambulance
4. skid in the sand
5. his leg will be as strong as it was before he broke it

Story 5

1. b
2. a
3. b
4. c
5. b
6. Answers will vary.

Unit 5. Food Store Words

Story 1

1. supermarket
2. bakery
3. frozen food aisle
4. get mixed up by the coupons and change
5. the manager will come talk to him
6. b

Story 2

1. Answers will vary.
2. corned beef
3. plastic number
4. someone else had driven off with her groceries
5. Answers will vary.

Story 3

1. c
2. b
3. c

4. a
5. b

Story 4

1. Answers will vary.
2. 1900
3. he asked them what he should buy

4. he can more quickly get just what he wants
5. he had invited all the kids in his class to come to a party

Story 5

1. tries to help his grandfather at the supermarket
2. a big gray coat
3. candy; put apples and lemons in the bag
4. he wouldn't have filled the tote bag with food
5. been covered with food

Unit 6. School Words

Story 1

1. a
2. b
3. c

4. c
5. a
6. Answers will vary.

Story 2

1. plan the bonfire and pep rally
2. talk to the principal and ask the teachers to come help that night
3. the band played some school songs
4. it will explode
5. "No, you may not."
6. Answers will vary.

Story 3

1. Dick and Eva are at this meeting to write a story about it for the school newspaper.
2. Dick and Eva talked to the computer teacher, Ms. Fry.
3. went to talk to the principal

4. There won't be another issue of the school newspaper because there won't be any money to pay for it.

5. They had just come up with the idea of doing their own newspaper.

Story 4

1. b   4. c
2. c   5. b
3. a

Story 5

Answers will vary.

1. a boy who goes to visit his new school   4. his mom got a new job in Maine
2. fire escape   5. Answers will vary.
3. showed him around the school   6. Answers will vary.

Unit 7. Health Words

Story 1

1. b   4. a
2. a   5. b
3. c

Story 2

1. a boy who has to have some teeth out
2. wisdom teeth
3. brushed his teeth; mouthwash
4. there isn't enough room for them in his mouth
5. (Answers will vary.) he had to have some teeth pulled

Story 3

1. b   4. b
2. c   5. a
3. a   6. Answers will vary.

Story 4

Answers will vary.

1. wants to help at the hospital
2. arm
3. phone call; hospital
4. sick
5. he likes helping other people

Story 5

1. a doctor who really helps people (Answers will vary.)
2. newspaper; hot soup
3. a man and a woman
4. Dr. Wanda yelled and threw herself at the woman and surprised her
5. she listens to their problems
6. Answers will vary.

Unit 8. Community Words

Story 1

1. b
2. c
3. b
4. a
5. a
6. Answers will vary.

Story 2

1. a
2. Scott's, Rocko's
3. synagogue
4. they wanted to have a lot of money themselves
5. they had a chance to go places and ask questions (Answers may vary.)
6. Answers will vary.

Story 3

1. c
2. a
3. c
4. c
5. b

Story 4

1. a
2. c
3. b
4. a
5. b

Story 5

1. studying town planning
2. the houses
3. decide where to make changes
4. there will be no place for playing fields
5. Answers will vary.
6. Maps will vary.

Unit 9. Restaurant Words

Story 1

1. two girls who went shopping and ate lunch in a restaurant
2. at a booth by the window
3. she ran into a waiter carrying a tray of dishes
4. dropped the tray
5. they were laughing (Answers may vary.)

Story 2

1. b
2. c
3. a
4. c
5. a
6. Answers will vary.

Story 3

1. Answers will vary.
2. Dean and Betty went to the Homestead Inn.
3. They called the waiter and ordered espresso.
4. Dean thinks there is always a long line in the ladies' room because the girls always have to go there together.
5. The girls skip the ladies' room to trick the boys.

Story 4

1. skipped school
2. it was too expensive
3. they went to a restaurant at the mall
4. they saw the principal and superintendent sitting by the door
5. Answers will vary.

Story 5

1. a, b, or c
2. must give a reason that supports 1
3. c
4. a
5. a
6. c

Unit 10. Travel Words

Story 1

1. b
2. a
3. c

4. b
5. Answers will vary.
6. Answers must support response to 5

Story 2

1. a girl who is learning to drive
2. the buses were loading, and the buses' lights were flashing
3. drove out toward the airport
4. slowed down and pulled over to the right
5. Answers will vary.

Story 3

1. b
2. b
3. a

4. c
5. c

Story 4

1. Answers will vary.
2. There were ten people in Kim's family on the boat.
3. They were going to a new country so they would be safe.
4. a church wanted to help them
5. Kim was happy because she had learned English and had wanted to go to North America for a long time. It would be a dream come true.
6. Answers will vary.

Story 5

1. has a day off from work and wants to do something daring
2. railroad bridge; river
3. map
4. he had been watching a boat and thinking about traveling somewhere
5. in his dream, he was almost in a train crash

Unit 1

Home Words

Story 1

The Costa family was moving from an apartment into a house. Tony, who was twelve, was very happy about this move. For the first time, he would have his own bedroom. His little brother, Rudy, would have his own room, too. They would share a bathroom in between their new rooms.

Tony and Rudy went with their mother when she got the key to the new house.

"Now the fun begins," Mrs. Costa said to the two boys. "We get to go look around at all the rooms."

"I can't wait to see mine," said Rudy. "Can we paint it dark blue?"

"I'm not sure what color to paint the rooms yet," said his mom.

"Who cares?" said Tony. "I want to see if we have space in the backyard to play baseball."

Mrs. Costa drove into the driveway. She stopped the car. She had a big smile on her face. She was very happy about her new home. The boys climbed out of the car. They ran around to the back of the house. Mrs. Costa started in the kitchen. One by one, she checked the stove, the refrigerator, and the washer and dryer. The family who lived there before had left a chair in the kitchen. She sat on the chair and looked at the cupboards. She decided the microwave would fit nicely under the left cupboard. She looked out the window. She could see the boys playing ball in the yard.

From the kitchen, she walked into the living room. On the far wall, she could see the wire for cable TV. She pictured how the rug and the couch would look. She decided to buy a new lamp for the living room. Before she went upstairs to look at the bedrooms, she called the boys inside.

"Let's go up and look at your rooms," she said.

(continued)

"I get the biggest one," said Tony.

"They're just alike, I think," his mom said.

The boys ran into the house. They beat their mom up the stairs. They ran down the hall and hid in a big closet.

"Shhh," said Tony. "Don't let Mom know where we're hiding."

"OK," said Rudy. But he started to giggle.

"Where are you, boys?" asked Mrs. Costa. No answer. She walked into the bathroom. She peeked into the bathtub. No sign of the boys. She noticed that the sink and toilet were white, but the bathtub was blue. That's funny, she thought.

"Come on, Rudy," she called. No answer. "I know you're here somewhere," she said. "I'll just have a look around." She looked in each bedroom. She checked the size of the closets. There was bright sunlight coming in the windows. She thought about shades and curtains. She made a list of things she wanted to buy. As she wrote, she walked down the hall to the rooms that would be the boys' bedrooms. She walked past the closet where the boys were hiding.

"Where are those kids?" she said out loud.

From behind her, the boys jumped out of the closet. "*Boo!*" they said.

Mrs. Costa screamed, dropping her list and her pencil. Before she could even turn around, Rudy and Tony had dashed down the stairs. They ran out to the car.

"Boy, did you see her jump?" Tony asked Rudy.

Rudy just laughed. "I think I like our new house," he said.

Story 1: Exercise

Fill in the blanks with the best answer.

1. **Main Idea:** Rudy and Tony have a new

   _____

2. **Details:** Rudy wants to paint his room

   _____

3. **Sequence:** Mrs. Costa looked around the kitchen. Then she went into the

   _____

4. **Cause and Effect:** The boys scared Mrs. Costa and she dropped

   _____

5. **Drawing Conclusions:** The boys liked their new house because

   _____

6. **Activity:** Write about your house or apartment.

   _____

   _____

   _____

Story 2

"Time for chores," called Mr. Rosen. "Nan! Sam! Turn off the video. Come into the kitchen."

"Be there in a minute, Pop," Sam yelled.

"I don't have all day," Mr. Rosen called back. "Nan, are you coming?"

"I'm on the phone. Just a minute."

Mrs. Rosen patted her husband on the back. "Don't worry. They'll come in a half hour or so. I'm going food shopping. See you later."

She smiled and took her car key off the key rack. "Don't forget to have Sam clean the bathroom. Good-bye, dear."

Mr. Rosen tapped his foot. Finally he walked into the living room and stood in front of the TV. "Sam," he said, "your job today is to clean the bathroom."

"Aw, Pop, do I have to? That's Nan's job."

"We're trading jobs today."

"Yuck. I hate cleaning the toilet and the bathtub."

"The cleaning stuff is under the sink. Do a good job. And get started *now*. We need to get the house cleaned while your mother is buying food."

Crossing the room, Mr. Rosen stopped behind Nan. She was still talking on the phone.

He tapped her on the shoulder. No answer. "Nan," he said in a loud voice. "Sign off now." He waited while she said good-bye to her friend. She turned around.

(continued)

5

"What is it, Dad?" Nan asked.

"I want you to clean the hall and the living room."

"That's not my job, Dad. That's Sam's job," Nan said. "I do the bathroom."

"Not today. Sam is doing the bathroom. I'm cleaning the refrigerator, the stove, and the microwave. And you're doing the living room."

"I hate doing the living room. Do I have to dust all Mom's little glass animals?"

 "'Fraid so. And dust the lamp, too. I got the vacuum cleaner out of the closet for you already. Be sure you vacuum under the couch and TV. And be careful not to pull on the cable wire."

"Yes, Dad," Nan said, looking unhappy. "I *was* going to put a load of wash in the washer."

"Oh," said her dad. "Go right ahead. I'll tell Sam to get his laundry together."

"Oh, brother. I have to do *all* the work around here," Nan muttered.

"If we all help, it will be done before you know it," her dad replied.

Story 2: Exercise

Circle the letter of the best answer.

1. **Main Idea:** This story tells about

    (a) teenagers at the Rosen's house

    (b) Mrs. Rosen going shopping

    (c) doing chores at the Rosen's house

2. **Details:** Mrs. Rosen wants

    (a) Nan to clean the bathroom

    (b) Sam to clean the bathroom

    (c) both children to clean their rooms

3. **Sequence:** Mr. Rosen told Nan to sign off. Then

    (a) he went downstairs

    (b) he turned off her tape player

    (c) he waited for her to say good-bye to her friend

4. **Cause and Effect:** Mr. Rosen said he would have Sam get his laundry because

    (a) Nan was going to start some laundry

    (b) his room was piled high with dirty clothes

    (c) it was Sam's job to do the laundry

5. **Drawing Conclusions:** If the children help Mr. Rosen, then

    (a) he will pay them

    (b) Mrs. Rosen will be happy

    (c) the work will be done quickly

6. **Activity:** Talk to someone else about chores you have to do at home.

7

Survival Vocabulary Stories

Story 3

Summer had just begun. But nothing much was happening. "I don't have anything to do," Sonya said to her mom.

"Why don't you try to get a job?" her mom asked.

"I don't think anyone will hire a fifteen-year-old," Sonya said.

"All you can do is try. If they think you're too young, they'll tell you," replied her mom.

Sonya looked in the newspaper every day to see if she could find a job. One day she saw an ad that said:

> **Wanted:** Person to clean apartments at the beach. Good pay. 20 hrs. per week. No experience needed. Call 921-3200.

Sonya rushed to the phone to call the number. A woman named Ms. Farid answered the phone. Ms. Farid said she would like to talk to Sonya at 1:00 that afternoon.

After she hung up, Sonya called her mom at work to tell her about her job interview.

When it was almost 1:00, Sonya rode her bike to Ms. Farid's house. Ms. Farid said she was happy to meet Sonya. The two of them talked for about fifteen minutes.

"Let's walk to the apartments," Ms. Farid said. "Then I can show you just what needs to be done."

"OK," said Sonya.

Ms. Farid explained that a family usually rented an apartment for a week. So, at the end of the week, someone had to get the apartment ready for the next family.

(continued)

Ms. Farid used a key to open the door to the apartment.

"First, get all the towels from the kitchen and the bathroom. Then, get the sheets from the bedroom. Take them downstairs to the basement. Put them in the washer and start it up." She pointed toward the basement stairs.

"All the cleaning supplies are kept in the basement closet," she said. "You'll have a kit there with your name on it. Get the kit and the vacuum cleaner, and carry them upstairs.

"The kitchen needs the most work," Ms. Farid said. "Spray some cleaner on the oven, and let it soak in. Meanwhile, clean out the refrigerator and empty the trash. Wipe the top of the stove and the microwave. Scrub the sink and the counters. Then go back and finish cleaning the oven. Finally, wash the kitchen floor."

"I can do all these things," said Sonya. "But where do I empty the trash?"

"There are cans in the closet out in the apartment hallway," Ms. Farid said.

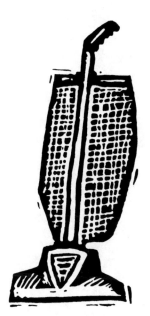

"Next, clean the bathroom. Scrub the toilet, the sink, and the bathtub. Then wash the bathroom floor," she said.

"While the floor is drying, go into the bedroom. Make the beds. Dust the furniture. And vacuum the rug. Last, dust and vacuum the living room," she said.

"Be sure to clean under the couch. Check the lamp to see that it works. And be careful around the cable TV wire. Now you're ready to start the next apartment," Ms. Farid said.

"Don't forget to put the wet laundry into the dryer when you go downstairs with the second set of towels and sheets."

"How many apartments do you want me to clean in one day?" Sonya asked. She was beginning to think that this looked like a pretty hard job.

(continued)

"I'm sure you'll be a bit slow at first. But we'll start you out working with someone else. You should be able to do three or four apartments in a day. Well, what do you think? Do you want the job?" she asked Sonya.

"I'm not sure," Sonya said. "How much do you pay per hour?"

"We start new workers at six dollars an hour," Ms. Farid said.

"OK," Sonya said. "I'd like to try it."

"Come back to my apartment. I'll give you a key," said Ms. Farid.

Sonya smiled all the way home. She was thinking about all the money she would earn. And she was happy she would have something to do for the summer.

Story 3: Exercise

Fill in the blanks with the best answer.

1. **Main Idea:** What is the one thing this story is about?

   _____

2. **Details:** What will Sonya have to do in the kitchen?

   _____

3. **Sequence:** What will Sonya do after she cleans the kitchen?

   _____

4. **Cause and Effect:** If Sonya is too young, Ms. Farid

   _____

5. **Drawing Conclusions:** Do you think Sonya was happy about her new job?

   _____

   Why do you think so?

   _____

6. **Activity:** Write about a job you have had. Say why you liked it or why you didn't like it.

   or

   Write about a job you would like to have. Why do you want this job?

Story 4

"This summer we're going to redo our kitchen," Mrs. Morin said. "And make an apartment in the basement," her husband added.

"I can't wait to start," said Mrs. Morin.

"First we need to draw up some plans," said Mr. Morin. "Guy, could you do that in your drafting class at school?"

"I could try," Guy said. "But I'll need to know what you want. What rooms do you want in the apartment? And where do you want things to go in the kitchen?"

"I have a lot of ideas for the kitchen," his mom said. "I know just where I want the stove, refrigerator, and sink to go. Suppose I sketch it out for you."

"Great," said Guy. "That will help." Mrs. Morin sat down at the kitchen table and started to draw.

"Dad, how about measuring the size of the kitchen, and also the basement," Guy suggested.

"Good idea. Let's start with the basement first." The two of them went down the basement stairs to begin.

Mrs. Morin tapped her pencil on the table. This was harder than she thought it would be. She wanted a closet in the kitchen for brooms and mops. She also wanted a place for the washer. But it didn't look like there was enough space the way the kitchen was set up now. Maybe she would have to use some space from the hall next to the kitchen. "I wonder," she said out loud. "What if we add on a little space to sit and eat. Then we can block off that doorway . . . ." She began to draw very fast.

When Guy and his dad came back upstairs, Mrs. Morin was beaming. "Look," she said. "I think I have come up with a great idea." She showed them her sketch. Mr. Morin raised one eyebrow.

(continued)

12

"That looks like it will cost a lot of money," he said. "How will we be able to afford both that and the basement apartment?"

"Well," said Mrs. Morin, "what are you planning for the apartment?"

"I think we want a small bedroom, a small bathroom, and a small living room. What do you think, Guy? Do we have enough space for those rooms in the basement?"

"I think so. But what about a kitchen? Won't someone who lives there want a kitchen?"

"Maybe just a small kitchen unit on one wall of the living room," his dad said. "The top of the unit could have a little sink and space for a microwave. The base could be a small refrigerator and some drawers. And in the bathroom, we can put in a shower instead of a bathtub. Can you sketch that out, Guy?"

Guy sat down beside his mother in a chair at the kitchen table. Soon, he had drawn three small rooms. In the living room he sketched a couch, a chair, and a lamp. At the bottom of the drawing, he added a key. The key showed which rooms would have rugs and which would have tile floors.

"That looks good, Guy. I wouldn't mind living down there," said his dad.

"You are good at drawing house designs," Mrs. Morin praised Guy. Then she turned to her husband and smiled. "If you say no to my new kitchen, you might find yourself living in that nice apartment!"

"Maybe I'd better take a closer look at your kitchen plan." Mr. Morin winked at Guy. They all laughed.

Story 4: Exercise

Fill in the blanks with the best answer.

1. **Main Idea:** A good title for this story would be

   _____

2. **Details:** The two things Mrs. Morin wanted in the kitchen were

   _____

3. **Sequence:** First, Mrs. Morin drew the kitchen. Then

   _____

   drew the plans for the

   _____

4. **Cause and Effect:** If Mr. Morin doesn't redo the kitchen the way Mrs. Morin wants it, then

   _____

5. **Drawing Conclusions:** Guy must have had a lot of practice drawing house plans, because

   _____

6. **Activity:** Draw a plan for redoing an area of your home.

   _____

Story 5

"Why does it have to rain on Saturday?" Kate grumbled to herself.

She was alone in the house. Her parents both had to work. She didn't have anything to do. She didn't have a car, so she couldn't go to the mall.

She lay on the couch in the living room and watched cable TV for a while. Then she switched to a video.

Finally she went to her bedroom to listen to some tapes. She knew she should do some homework. But she didn't want to.

When she heard a knock at the door, she jumped up. She ran down the stairs. She looked through the little peephole in the door to see who was there.

Her face lit up. A bunch of her friends stood outside the front door. They were calling, "Hey Kate! Let us in! We're not getting any drier out here in the rain!"

She turned the key to shut off the alarm system. "Come on in," she said, opening the door wide. "You can hang your wet coats here in the hall closet. Oh, and put your umbrellas in the bathtub in the downstairs bathroom."

"That's a weird idea," said one of the boys.

"Well, that way they won't drip all over my mom's good rug," said Kate.

Before the last coat was hung in the closet, someone called from the kitchen, "Hey, what have you got to eat, Kate? I'm starved."

"Me, too," said someone else.

Kate could hear the refrigerator door open and close. "Gee," said Kate. "Why don't you make yourselves at home?"

(continued)

"We're trying," her friend Jade answered. "We were bored. So we thought we'd get a gang together to spend the afternoon. We knew your house would be better than my mom's apartment."

"I'm so glad you came over," Kate said. "I was going nuts."

"Let's make some popcorn and hot cocoa," said Jade.

By the time they got to the kitchen, the boys had cocoa heating on the stove. "Good work, guys," Kate said. "I didn't know you had these cooking skills."

Bob laughed. "Want to see me make popcorn in the microwave? I really know my way around the kitchen."

"Not me," said Chuck. "I barely know how to open a can, unless it's a can of soda."

"Speaking of soda," Maya said, "do you mind if I have some?"

"No, that's OK," said Kate. She took a big bottle out of the refrigerator and handed it to Maya.

Maya put the bottle on the kitchen table. As she started to twist the top off, the soda began to fizz.

Then it happened. The soda shot out of the bottle. It hit the lamp over the table and rained down on the tablecloth and on Maya.

Maya screamed and ran to the kitchen sink. She leaned over the sink. Soda dripped from her face and hair. When the other kids stopped laughing, they grabbed paper towels and started to soak up the soda.

"Don't worry," said Kate. "We can clean this up." Just as she said that, the popcorn began to pop in the microwave. The kids were so busy cleaning up the soda, they didn't pay attention to the popping.

"Uh-oh," said Bob, as the smell of the burning popcorn reached him. "So much for my kitchen skills." He ran to turn off the microwave. The package inside had began to turn black. He had forgotten to time the popcorn.

(continued)

Kate was standing on a chair wiping the soda off the lamp. She reached into the cupboard for a bowl for the popcorn.

"Here," she said. She leaned over the stove to hand the bowl to Bob. She thought *he* had ahold of the bowl. He thought *she* still did. As a result, the bowl dropped right onto the pot of hot cocoa. Cocoa splashed out all over the top of the stove and down the front of Kate's shirt.

"I give up!" Kate shouted with laughter. "This kitchen must be jinxed. What *else* can happen?" She collapsed in the chair.

"Don't ask!" Jade said.

"I'll never complain about rainy Saturdays again," Kate said. "Thank you all for making my day so exciting."

❖

Story 5: Exercise

Circle the letter of the best answer.

1. **Main Idea:** This story is about

    (a) a rainy Saturday at Kate's house

    (b) after school one day

    (c) Kate's birthday party

2. **Details:** When Kate went to the door, she saw

    (a) her mom and dad

    (b) her cousins

    (c) her friends

3. **Sequence:** First the boys made the cocoa, then

    (a) Maya opened the bottle of soda

    (b) Bob smelled the popcorn burning in the microwave

    (c) the kids hung up their coats

4. **Cause and Effect:** The popcorn got overcooked because

    (a) no one was timing it

    (b) the popper broke

    (c) Bob forgot to put a bowl to catch the popcorn

5. **Drawing Conclusions:** If Kate's parents walked in right now

    (a) they would be upset

    (b) they wouldn't notice the mess

    (c) they would say hi to Kate's friends

    Explain why you answered the way you did.

    _____

6. **Activity:** Write about what you do on rainy Saturdays.

Food Words

Story 1

The whole ninth-grade class was planning to go on a three-day camping trip. First, the kids chose the friends they wanted in their tent. Then it was time to talk about the food for the trip. The kids in each tent had to plan what food to take with them. They had a class meeting in the gym with Ms. Yung, the teacher in charge.

"Now students," said Ms. Yung, "for breakfast you will want some food that is easy to fix, like cereal."

"Are we supposed to bring milk?" asked Jon.

"How about sugar?" Anna asked.

"You can buy milk at the camp store. But you should bring some sugar," Ms. Yung replied. "You might also want fruit for breakfast. Oranges and apples are good camping foods."

"I want to cook pancakes over a campfire," said Boris.

"Yeah, me too," said Jon. "Don't forget the butter and maple syrup."

"Or maybe eggs and bacon," said Anna. "Mmmm. I'm hungry just thinking about it."

"Do you think we'll need coffee or tea?" Boris asked.

"I'd rather drink juice and hot cocoa. Don't forget the marshmallows," Anna said.

"Let's not go too fast," said Ms. Yung. "We're still talking about breakfast. We still have snacks, lunch, and dinner to talk about."

"For a snack, let's have soda and cookies," Jon said.

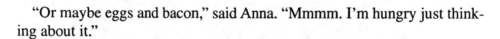

(continued)

"Now wait a minute," Ms. Yung said. "Your snack should give you energy. But it shouldn't have too much sugar in it. Something like raisins and nuts would be good."

"I never eat anything like that," said Anna. "I bet you want us to eat stuff like bread and water. Yuck!"

"But you do need water while you're hiking," said Ms. Yung. "And you need bread if you're going to have sandwiches for lunch."

"How about some dry soup to mix with hot water?" Lynn asked.

"You could have some soup at supper," Ms. Yung answered. "But we'll be hiking up a mountain at noon. So we won't have any hot water at lunchtime."

"I know," said Anna. "We could bring meat and vegetables and make stew for supper."

"I want hot dogs. That's all I know how to cook," said Todd.

Breakfast
fresh Orange juice, fluffy eggs, ham, coffee Cake, Cocoa and Marshmallows
Lunch
Chips, Soda, Cookies, and Candy bars
Dinner
Pancakes, Maple Syrup, Cake, and Chocolate Milk Shakes
Snacks
(one each hour)
Candy, Chips, Soda

"Let's get into our tent groups," said Ms. Yung. "We need to plan food for the whole trip." There was a lot of noise as the students moved around the room and got into groups.

Jon, Boris, and Todd were in one group. They wrote list after list of meals. Finally they came up with one that made them all happy.

"Ms. Yung, Ms. Yung," Jon called out. "I think we're done."

"Come look," said Todd, with a sly grin. "I think you will agree that we have included nothing but healthy food on our menu." He handed the paper to Ms. Yung. She shook her head as she read it.

(continued)

"Breakfast looks fine," she said. "But the rest of it . . ." She frowned. "You should take this plan home to talk over with your parents. We'll see if *they* think it's a good one."

The boys started to laugh. Ms. Yung looked up from the list.

"Just kidding, Ms. Yung," Jon said. "Here's our *real* plan for meals."

He handed her a piece of paper with neatly written meal plans.

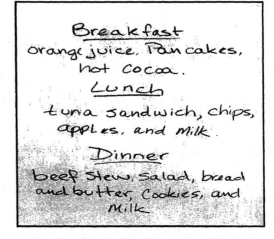

Here is what they planned for the first day:

Breakfast: orange juice
               pancakes
               hot cocoa

Lunch: tuna sandwich
               chips
               apples
               milk

Dinner: beef stew
               salad
               bread and butter
               cookies
               milk

"Now you're cooking!" said Ms. Yung.

"Whoa," said Todd. "If only we could bring someone along to cook for us."

❖

        Survival Vocabulary Stories

Name _____

Date _____

Story 1: Exercise

Circle the letter of the best answer.

1. **Main Idea:** A good title for this story would be

    (a) Boris and Jon Plan Meals

    (b) The Ninth Grade Goes Camping

    (c) Planning for a Camping Trip

2. **Details:** Boris wanted to cook

    (a) fried eggs

    (b) pancakes

    (c) ham

3. **Sequence:** First, Ms. Yung talked to the students. Then

    (a) the students got into groups

    (b) the boys went to one room

    (c) the students went back to class

4. **Cause and Effect:** The boys made a bad meal plan. Then

    (a) Ms. Yung called the principal

    (b) Ms. Yung shook her head and frowned

    (c) Ms. Yung sent the plan home

5. **Drawing Conclusions:** If the boys didn't have a good meal plan,

    (a) they would have to stay home

    (b) they would have to make up a new one

    (c) they would be hungry on the camping trip

Story 2

All the ninth-graders were up before dawn. They packed a few last-minute things. Then they rushed to get to school by 6:00 A.M. The day to start out on the class camping trip had finally arrived.

The students loaded their sleeping bags, tents, and coolers full of food into pickup trucks. Jon, Boris, and Todd had one of the biggest coolers.

"Boy, is this thing heavy," Boris said. He tried to lift it into the back of the truck. "We only need food for three days."

"Well," said Todd, "we have all those vegetables and fruits that Ms. Yung told us to bring. Plus we added a few cans of soda." He winked at Jon. "Our snacks will be the best in camp!"

"I think our breakfasts will be best," said Jon. "I can almost taste those pancakes now."

"I just hope you can cook," Todd said. "I've never flipped a pancake in my life."

"This will be a good time to learn," said Ms. Yung. She was walking from group to group, helping students load their things. "As soon as your stuff is loaded, go get on the bus. I think we're ready to leave."

The school buses bumped and rattled up the old road into the mountains. Some of the kids listened to portable tape and CD players. Others talked. And some sang songs. After about an hour, Jon said, "I think it must be snack time. I hope you all put food into your backpacks." He reached under his seat for his pack.

"I've got mine," said Todd.

"Here's mine," said Boris. "What have you got, Todd?"

"Juice boxes and cookies. How about you?"

(continued)

"From the way it smells, I think my mom packed some egg sandwiches for me." Boris said. "Oh, *no*. They're all flat from being on the bottom of my pack." He pulled out two very thin sandwiches.

"That must be your lunch," Todd said. "Or I should say, that *was* your lunch."

"I need my sugar," said Jon. "I hope I have some soda in here." He reached into his pack. "Oh *great*," he said. "My mom put in a canteen of water and some small boxes of cereal."

"So far, our food plans haven't worked out," said Todd. "Things can only get better. What are we supposed to have for supper tonight?"

"Tonight it's chicken. I think we have carrot sticks for our vegetable and milk to drink," Jon said.

"There's not much we can do to ruin that," said Todd. Later, after he had eaten the burned chicken wings which had fallen into the fire, he decided he had been wrong. The boys went over to check out what Anna and Lynn had cooked. Their stew looked like watery soup.

"This could be a *long* three days," Boris said. "I could really go for a bowl of ice cream right about now."

"Don't even talk about ice cream," said Jon. "Just keep your mind set on those pancakes that Todd is going to cook for breakfast."

Todd didn't say anything. When they got back to their tent, he took out the box of pancake mix and read the directions. He went to sleep dreaming about giant pancakes.

In the morning, a heavy rain was falling. "Guess we can't make pancakes," said Todd. "We'll never get a fire going in this rain."

"We don't need to build a fire. I brought a gas camping stove," said Jon.

"Oh," said Todd. He read the back of the pancake box once again. "OK. I guess I'm ready. Here goes nothing." He poured some mix into a bowl. He

(continued)

added an egg and some water. Then he stirred for a while. He melted some butter in the pan. Carefully he poured the pancake batter into small circles. In a moment, the pancakes began to smoke.

"Hey, Jon! How do you turn this thing down?" Todd called out.

"You don't," said Jon. "Just turn the pancakes over real fast." Todd flipped the pancakes as fast as he could. But already they were black on one side. In a few minutes, he took the pancakes out of the pan and put them on paper plates. The other sides of the pancakes were burned, too.

"Mmmm," said Boris. "These smell pretty good." The boys put butter and syrup on their pancakes. They all took big bites. Then they looked at each other with their mouths full of pancakes.

Todd was the first one to choke down his mouthful. "Oh yuck," he said. "The middle isn't cooked, and the outside is burned. These taste awful."

"You said it," Jon said. He took a big drink of milk. "Let's try some cold cereal."

Just then the boys heard a whistle blow. They knew it was time to start the day's activities. Boris went canoeing. Jon and Todd went hiking. They planned to meet back at their tent just before supper. Jon and Todd got back first. Boris didn't show up until much later. When he did, his finger was all bandaged up.

"What happened?" Todd and Jon asked at the same time.

"Looks like I broke my finger when I fell out of the canoe," Boris said.

"Oh, *no*," said Todd. "Do you have to go home and miss the rest of the camping trip?"

"Yeah, but here's the *good* thing," said Boris. "I get to eat *real* food. You guys get to eat burned chicken and raw pancakes!"

Story 2: Exercise

Fill in the blanks with the best answer.

1. **Main Idea:** This story is about

   _____

2. **Details:** Boris had

   _____

   for his snack. Todd had

   _____

3. **Sequence:** After the kids loaded their stuff on the truck, they

   _____

4. **Cause and Effect:** Boris's sandwiches were flat because

   _____

5. **Drawing Conclusions:** Todd wasn't very good at cooking pancakes because

   _____

6. **Activity:** Write about one time when you cooked something.

   _____

   _____

Story 3

"Who can tell us about the food pyramid?" Mr. Millo asked his tenth-grade health class.

Jake looked over at Al and shook his head. "Another boring class," he whispered.

"Jake, did you have something to say?" Mr. Millo asked. "Maybe you can name the six sections of the food pyramid."

"Uh, let me see." Jake looked around the class, hoping for some help. "I don't really know. Maybe cookies, soda, burgers. . . ." The class laughed.

Mr. Millo laughed, too. "Not a bad guess, Jake. But it sounds like you need some food facts."

"I wouldn't want him to plan *my* meals," said Paula. "What happened to fruits and vegetables, Jake?"

"And how about meat and milk?" Zeb asked.

"Well, I was close," Jake said. "There is meat in a burger. And some soda has fruit juice and sugar in it."

"I could go for some burgers right now," said Tom, the largest boy in the class. The class laughed again. Kids began to talk about how hungry they were and how they wished they had a snack.

(continued)

"Class, settle down," Mr. Millo said. "Let's get back to the lesson. In fact, let's get back to Jake's hamburger."

"I wish I could," said Jake.

"A hamburger goes in another food group as well as the meat/protein group. Anyone know what it is?"

"The roll," Kelly said. "I think it's the bread group. Or is it cereal?"

"Actually," said Mr. Millo. "it's the grain group." He pulled out a folder full of pictures of food. "Here are some pictures of every-day foods. See if you can make a food pyramid."

The class worked in small groups for about ten minutes. When they finished, they found that they had piled the food pictures into groups of fruits, vegetables, proteins, grains, dairy products, and fats/sugars.

"So where do you put water?" Jake asked. "My mom is always telling me I should drink more water."

"It's important," said Mr. Millo, "but it doesn't go in any of these groups. Same with coffee and tea. They're mostly water. Where did you put eggs, Kelly?"

"I put them in with milk things. But I don't think that's right."

"Usually they're in with meat, fish, poultry, beans, and nuts, because they give you protein," Mr. Millo said.

"Does anyone know why there are so many pictures in the grain group?" Mr. Millo asked.

(continued)

Survival Vocabulary Stories

"Because we should eat more servings from that group?" Paula asked.

"Right, Mr. Millo said. "Grains form the base of the pyramid."

"It looks like we should eat the least number of servings from the fats/sugar group then," Zeb said.

"You've got it," said Mr. Millo.

"Butter belongs with milk, though, doesn't it?" Kelly asked.

"I'd put it in the fats/sugar group," said Mr. Millo.

"I think it belongs with pancakes and maple syrup," Tom said. "I could eat that for breakfast, lunch, and supper. I would never get tired of it."

"That's on days when you're not eating burgers for breakfast, lunch, and supper," said Jake. The class laughed. But then the bell rang, saving Tom from trying to answer.

❖

Story 3: Exercise

Fill in the blanks with the best answer.

1. **Main Idea:** A good title for this story is

   _____

2. **Details:** The class is learning about

   _____

3. **Sequence:** First, the class talked about the food groups. Then

   _____

4. **Cause and Effect:** Jake whispered to Al. Then

   _____

5. **Drawing Conclusions:** Tom may be the largest boy in the class because

   _____

6. **Activity:** Make a chart and keep a list of the food you eat for a week.
   Do you eat foods from all six sections of the food pyramid?

   _____

   _____

   _____

   _____

Story 4

"Maria, you look as thin as a postage stamp," Mrs. Smith said. "Are you sure you're eating the right foods?"

"Of course, Mom. You know what I eat, anyway. You're the one who fixes my supper. And I eat the same breakfast you do," Maria replied. She helped herself to a handful of cookies. Her mother looked puzzled.

"Why don't you write down everything you eat for the next few days. I'm worried about you. You always seem to be eating snacks. But you're not gaining weight. What did you have for lunch today?" Mrs. Smith asked. As she talked, she tied an apron around her waist. She got the fish for supper out of the freezer.

Maria sat down at the kitchen table. She took a piece of paper out of her notebook. "Why don't I make a list of the food I've eaten today. Then maybe you'll stop worrying," she said, smiling at her mother.

"I'll make a cup of tea while we talk," Mrs. Smith said. She put a mug of hot water in the microwave.

"First, for breakfast, I had a bowl of cereal with milk and sugar and a glass of orange juice. At school for lunch, I had a bowl of soup and an egg salad sandwich on rye bread. How am I doing so far?"

"So far that sounds good. Now you've just had cookies for a snack. How about a piece of fruit, maybe an apple, before you start your homework?" Mrs. Smith asked.

"I'd rather have some coffee cake with butter on it and a glass of soda," Maria said.

 Mrs. Smith began to fix the vegetables for supper. She shook her head. "Listening to what you eat, I should be worried that you are going to weigh a ton. If I ate like you do . . ."

"Oh, Mom. I'm just a growing teenager, that's all. I'm really not losing weight. I'm just getting

(continued)

taller," Maria said. She helped herself to a large piece of coffee cake. "But you know, I'm really upset about my friend Dee."

"Why? She's such a nice girl."

"She is. But she goes for days without eating, to try to be thin. Then she really pigs out. After that, she makes herself throw up. Isn't that really bad for you?" Maria asked.

"Yes, it is. It's usually a sign of a person who needs a lot of help. Have you tried to talk to her about it?"

"Yes. But she doesn't want to admit that there's a problem. She just laughs it off. Do you think there's something I can do to help her, Mom?"

"Keep on being her friend. Try to get her to talk to her family about the problem. Suggest that she go talk to the school nurse. She needs to get help before her problem gets worse."

"She could die, couldn't she, if she doesn't stop?" Maria asked.

"Yes, she could. Do you want me to call up her mother?"

"I doubt it would do any good. Dee thinks her mom doesn't care about her at all. Her mom is always busy with Dee's little sister, who is a super ice skater. The two of them are always at the ice rink. Dee is usually at home alone."

"So, that's part of her problem. Why don't you ask Dee to come home with you in the afternoon. Maybe the two of us can begin to talk to her and get her some help."

"Thanks, Mom." Maria gave her mother a big hug. "Well, got to go do homework. Mind if I take this bag of chips upstairs with me?"

"Maybe your good appetite will rub off on Dee after she watches you eat every afternoon," Mrs. Smith said.

"I don't need any help eating my chips," Maria smiled as she ran upstairs.

Story 4: Exercise

Circle the letter of the best answer.

1. **Main Idea:** A good title for this story is

   (a) Maria's Mom Is Worried

   (b) After-School Talk

   (c) Maria Has a Snack

2. **Details:** While Mrs. Smith and Maria talk, Mrs. Smith drinks some

   (a) soda

   (b) coffee

   (c) tea

3. **Sequence:** First they talk about what Maria eats. Then

   (a) they talk about Maria's friend Dee

   (b) they talk about dinner

   (c) they talk about what's on cable TV

4. **Cause and Effect:** Dee may have an eating problem because

   (a) she eats too much

   (b) she doesn't have any friends

   (c) she is lonely

5. **Drawing Conclusions:** Mrs. Smith is worried about Maria because

   (a) she eats a lot of junk food

   (b) she eats a lot but doesn't gain weight

   (c) she doesn't have any friends

Survival Vocabulary Stories

Story 5

Ryan noticed that his new friend Nor wasn't eating much lunch.

Nor mostly just sat and looked at the meat loaf, vegetables, and bread and butter. Every now and then he ate a bit of the vegetables. But then he always took a big drink of water, as if he didn't like what he was eating.

Nor was from Cambodia. He didn't speak much English.

Ryan decided to try to find out if something was bothering Nor.

"What's the matter, Nor? Aren't you hungry?" Ryan asked.

"Yes, hungry. But I don't know this food," Nor said.

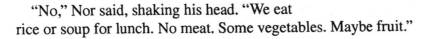

"Oh," said Ryan. "Don't you have this meat in your country?"

"No," Nor said, shaking his head. "We eat rice or soup for lunch. No meat. Some vegetables. Maybe fruit."

"This must be hard for you," Ryan said. "I've never been to another country. So I didn't think about the food being so different. Do you drink tea or coffee in Cambodia?"

"I drink tea. No coffee and not much milk. No cereal from a box. No cookies."

"Wow," Ryan said. "I can't think what it would be like not to have *cookies*. What about soda and snacks?"

"Some soda in cities. No people eat snacks. Just eat a lot of breakfast, lunch, and supper."

(continued)

Nor smiled at Ryan. "You think Cambodian food strange. I think American food strange. Yes?"

"I'd like to try some Cambodian food sometime. Maybe you could make some for our class one day. How about egg fried rice? I had that in a restaurant once," Ryan said.

Nor laughed. "That is Chinese food, I think."

"Oh," Ryan laughed, too. "Same part of the world, I guess."

He ate some of his meat loaf. "Here, put some ketchup on yours. I think you'll like it—it's a lot like a hamburger."

Nor watched what Ryan did. Then he tried some meat loaf with ketchup. "Not bad," he said.

All at once, with Ryan for a friend, Nor felt better about living in the United States.

"Maybe I like your food," Nor said, trying another bite.

❖

Name _____

Date _____

Story 5

Fill in the blanks with the best answer.

1. **Main Idea:** This story is about

   _____

2. **Details:** In his former country, Nor ate

   _____ for lunch.

3. **Sequence:** First, Ryan saw that Nor wasn't eating. Then

   _____

4. **Cause and Effect:** After Nor put ketchup on his meat,

   _____

5. **Drawing Conclusions:** Nor felt better about living in the United States because

   _____

Unit 3

Family Words

Story 1

Lee Chin was born in China. When Lee was twelve years old, he and his mother packed up and got ready to leave China. His mother was going to study at a college in Canada for a year.

Lee said good-bye to his father. He also said good-bye to his grandmother and his grandfather. He felt both sad and happy about leaving. He knew he wouldn't see his family for a whole year.

Lee and his mother boarded the airplane. "Look, Lee," his mother said. "Your father is waving to us." She waved to her husband. She tried to smile. But she knew she would miss him very much.

Seeing his mother smile made Lee feel better. He waved and smiled, too. The plane rolled down the runway.

As the plane took off, Lee's mother said, "Before you know it, we'll be in Vancouver with Aunt Lin and Uncle Fan."

"I've never met them," said Lee. "Do they have a son or daughter near my age?"

"Yes," his mother said. "They have a daughter, your cousin Ann. She is a year younger than you. I haven't seen her since she was a baby. In fact, I haven't seen my sister, Aunt Lin, for ten years."

"That's a long time," said Lee. "Do you think you'll know her when we get to the airport?" He sounded worried.

His mother laughed. "Of course I will. She looks like me. But her hair is longer." She patted her short black hair. "My sister's hair is down to here," she said. She pointed to her shoulders. "Also, she will be wearing the red silk dress I sent her for her birthday."

(continued)

Lee sat back. "I wish I had a sister or a brother," he said. "I won't have anyone to do things with."

"Your cousin will take you to school and show you the city. It will be almost like having a sister."

The airplane trip lasted the whole day. Lee grew very sleepy. Finally he fell asleep.

He began to dream about his family. He dreamed that it was the New Year. All over China, families were meeting for parties.

In his dream, he had an older brother. He was one year older than Lee. The two boys wore dragon masks. They marched in a children's parade. The other children in the parade were his father's nieces and nephews.

In the dream, his father had a new wife with long black hair. Lee didn't like this stepmother. The parade ended. The family sat down at a huge table to eat dinner. Lee could smell rice and pork and egg rolls. He was so hungry. He woke up with a start.

His mother was patting him on the arm. "It's time to have dinner. Smell the good pork and rice," she said.

Lee smiled as he thought about his dream and his family.

Story l: Exercise

Fill in the blanks with the best answer.

1. **Main Idea:** Lee is going on a long _____. He will miss his

   _____

2. **Details:** Lee's Aunt Lin will be wearing a

   _____

3. **Sequence:** After Lee dreamed about the parade, he dreamed

   _____

4. **Cause and Effect:** If Aunt Lin wears a red silk dress, then

   _____

5. **Drawing Conclusions:** If Lee had a brother or sister, then

   _____

6. **Title:** The best title for the story is
   (a) A Plane Trip
   (b) Lee Misses His Family
   (c) Lee Takes a Trip

Story 2

Grandmother Jones had a big family. She had two sons and three daughters of her own. And she was a guardian to another boy. Each of her children had been married and had children. Grandmother had ten grandchildren.

On holidays, the family liked to be together. For Thanksgiving dinner, Grandmother made three pumpkin pies and two apple pies. She cooked a turkey and a ham.

Each son and each daughter brought food, too. Everyone ate too much.

After the meal, all the nieces and nephews played touch football. Their parents sat and talked. There were lots of dishes to wash.

By the time Grandmother Jones was ninety years old, some of her grandchildren were married. She had nine great-grandchildren. The family decided to have a big birthday party for Grandmother. Her birthday was the same day as the birthday of the United States, July 4.

Who had a big enough house for all the Joneses? One granddaughter said she could fit all of the aunts and uncles in her house. Everyone else could sleep outside in tents.

She made a big chart showing which aunts and uncles would sleep in which room. She found space for eighteen people in the house. She saved the nicest guest room for Grandmother.

Next, the granddaughter wrote letters inviting each of her cousins and their families to come. She asked them to bring food and paper plates and cups. No one in the family liked to wash a lot of dishes.

(continued)

She also asked them to make a square for a quilt. And inside each envelope she put a plain white square of fabric. The square could be designed to show something about the family who made it. The quilt would be a surprise present for Grandmother.

As the days went by, the squares for the quilt came back to the granddaughter. She began to sew the quilt together.

One square showed the family riding in a big orange bus. The family dog had his head out the bus window. Grandmother had always liked that dog.

Another square was made to look like the front page of a newspaper. It told all about the family party for Grandmother.

One family stitched sailboats. Another one painted a picture of their house.

On the day of the party, all the aunts, uncles, cousins, nieces and nephews, sons and daughters, and husbands and wives came to the party. They put their food in the kitchen. Then, one by one, they set up their tents.

Soon, there were small children playing in a wading pool. Big children played table tennis. Grown-ups sat and talked with Grandmother. They laughed about some good times at her house.

Finally, after dinner, the big moment came. It was time to give Grandmother her quilt. The granddaughter who put it all together gave Grandmother a big hug.

"We have a surprise for you," she said. Gently she unfolded the quilt and placed it in Grandmother's lap. She showed Grandmother how each family had helped to make the quilt.

Grandmother was so happy, she couldn't think of a thing to say. She kept looking at the different squares, and touching the one in the middle of the quilt. Neatly stitched into the middle square were the words "We love you."

Story 2: Exercise

Choose the best answer.

1. **Main Idea:** This story is about

   (a) the Jones family

   (b) a birthday party for Grandmother Jones

   (c) how to make a quilt

2. **Details:** Grandmother's granddaughter found space for _____ people to sleep in the house.

3. **Sequence:** As soon as she knew she had enough space for everyone, the granddaughter

   (a) sent letters inviting her cousins to come

   (b) started baking cookies

   (c) started to make the quilt

4. **Cause and Effect:** If everyone brings paper plates and paper cups, then

   (a) they can have a picnic

   (b) it will cost a lot of money

   (c) no one will have to do a lot of dishes

5. **Drawing Conclusions:** Grandmother must have liked her quilt, because

   (a) she cried when she saw it

   (b) she kept touching the square that said "We love you."

   (c) she hugged her granddaughter

6. **Activity:** Ask your grandparents to tell you about a party they remember. Write down what they tell you.

Story 3

Mr. and Mrs. Ford decided this was the year to take a trip across country. The Summer Olympics were being held in California. The Fords lived in Vermont. They could stop on their way to the Olympic Games to visit their family and relatives. If they left home when school ended in June, they could be at the Olympics by August 1.

"First," Mrs. Ford said, "we must write to Aunt Sue and Uncle Jack in New York to see when we can visit them."

"After New York, we could head south to Alabama and visit my sister and her new baby," said Mr. Ford. "Right," said his wife. "I'll call my brother George in Iowa to find out if he has room for us to stay with him."

"Don't forget I have a cousin in Idaho," her husband said. "Maybe we could stay with her for a while, too."

"I'm getting excited about this trip," said Mrs. Ford. "Let's ask the children to help plan it."

"Good idea," said Mr. Ford. "Steve, Sharon, come here, please." Steve, who was fourteen, and Sharon, who was fifteen, pulled themselves away from the video they were watching.

"What's up?" Sharon asked.

"We thought you might want to help plan our trip across country to go to the Olympic Games in California." her father said.

"California! Wow. Really?" said Steve. "Cool," said Sharon. "I think we should stop at the Baseball Hall of Fame in Cooperstown, New York. And we just have to go to a Dodgers game while we're in Los Angeles."

"No," groaned Steve. "I don't want to do that. I want to see the Grand Canyon and go on a raft down the Mississippi River."

(continued)

"Hold it," Mrs. Ford said to her son and daughter. "Each of you may make a list of places you want to visit. We plan to visit some of your cousins and aunts and uncles. If we can, we'll stop to see some famous places."

"What about Grandfather Ford? Will we see him, too?" Sharon asked. "I bet he'd like to go to a ball game with us." She gave her brother a dirty look.

"Yes. We'll visit him and my stepmother. But I don't think we'll have time to go to a ball game," her mother answered. "We'll want to have a lot of time to see Olympic events."

"Steve," Mr. Ford said to his son, "here is some information about campsites. See which ones look like good places to stay. Then let Sharon look. We're going to go down south on our way out and come back across the northern part of the country. Sharon, here is the Olympics schedule. Choose four or five events you'd like to see. Then give the information to Steve so he can choose some, too."

"We have to order Olympics tickets soon," said Mrs. Ford, "or we won't get them in time."

The children went to their rooms to study the information. Before long their parents could hear them arguing about what they would do and where they would stay.

"Maybe we should have planned this by ourselves," Mr. Ford said with a smile. "We may end up with a major war on our hands. I'll call my stepfather and see if he can mow the lawn while we're gone."

"Good. I'll ask my niece to pick up the mail and feed the dog and cat," Mrs. Ford said. "Do you think your nephew would weed the garden?"

"I'll ask him. Sure is a lot of work to get ready for a trip." Mr. Ford went to the telephone. Mrs. Ford began to make lists of things to do to get ready to go. Upstairs, Sharon and Steve were still arguing.

Story 3: Exercise

Circle the letter of the best answer.

1. **Main Idea:** This story tells about

    (a) the Ford family on a trip

    (b) the Ford family after a trip

    (c) the Ford family planning a trip

2. **Details:** Mr. Ford said

    (a) the children could not help plan the trip

    (b) he would ask his stepfather to mow the lawn

    (c) he wanted to go to a baseball game

3. **Sequence:** After Sharon chooses some events,

    (a) she will give the Olympics information to Steve

    (b) she will send for tickets

    (c) she will mow the lawn

4. **Cause and Effect:** If the Fords want to see the Olympics,

    (a) then they will have no money left to see a baseball game

    (b) then they will have to order tickets soon

    (c) then they will have to call Grandfather Ford

5. **Drawing Conclusions:** If the children continue to argue,

    (a) they may not get to help plan the trip

    (b) they will have to weed the garden

    (c) they won't get to go on the trip

6. **Activity:** Write about a trip you took with your family or with a friend.

Story 4

Carl and Sara were standing in line to get graduation tickets for their families.

"I hope I can get as many tickets as I need," Carl said.

"How many do you need?" Sara asked.

"About twenty," said Carl.

"How come so many?" asked Sara.

"My family is hard to explain," Carl said. "I have two mothers, two fathers, four grandmothers, and four grandfathers."

"Wow! How many brothers and sisters do you have?" Sara asked.

"I have two real brothers and two half sisters who live with me. Then I have two half brothers who live at my father's. My real father's, that is."

"Do I dare ask you how many cousins you have?" Sara asked again.

"You can ask me," Carl grinned, "but I can't count that high. My mother gave up trying to keep track of her nieces and nephews years ago. Let's just put it this way. After my graduation, we have to rent a hall to have room for all my family."

"I'm an only child," said Sara. "I live with a woman who is my guardian. I don't know what it would be like to have all those people in one family. Is it fun?"

(continued)

"It's a big mess when it comes to things like graduation. But I guess it's OK. We all get along pretty well."

"You don't really have two mothers and two fathers, do you?" Sara asked.

"Well, I have a mother and a stepmother. And I have a father and a stepfather. That's a lot of parents to have to deal with," Carl answered. "What about you? What's it like to be an only child?"

"I don't mind it. At least I don't have to share my room with anybody. But sometimes I get lonely," Sara said.

"Just come over to my house. You'll never be lonely. Sometimes I could use some peace and quiet," Carl said.

"It sure would be fun to have a sister or a brother to do things with," Sara said. "I do have a few cousins. They are the children of my guardian's sister. But they live far away. I only get to see them when we have a family get-together."

"Maybe you should join our family," Carl said. "We've got sons and daughters and husbands and wives to spare. Can you imagine if my mother and stepfather got a divorce and then each one remarried?"

"That would be too much," Sara agreed.

"I'd need a giant chart to figure out who was who," Carl laughed.

"It's almost my turn to get tickets. Want me to get as many as I can, then give the extra ones to you?" Sara asked.

"That would be great," Carl said. "I'll need all the extras I can get my hands on!"

Story 4: Exercise

Fill in the blanks with the best answer.

1. **Main Idea:** Carl and Sara need _____ for graduation.

2. **Details:** Sara is a(n) _____ child.

3. **Details:** Carl needs about _____ tickets.

4. **Sequence:** First, Sara will get her tickets. Then _____ will get his tickets.

5. **Drawing Conclusions:** If Sara shares her tickets with Carl, then

_____

6. **Title:** The best title for the story is

   (a) Graduation Day

   (b) Carl's Big Family

   (c) Tickets to a Play

Story 5

School was finally over. The day arrived for the Fords to start their trip across the United States to see the Summer Olympics. Their van was packed and ready to go.

Mrs. Ford's niece came over to say good-bye and play with the dog and cat. Mr. Ford's stepfather came to put gas in the lawn mower and say good-bye. And Mr. Ford's nephew came to see if the garden needed weeding. All the neighbors waved as the Fords' van drove slowly down the street.

"Do you think we have everything?" Mrs. Ford asked.

"If we don't, it's too late now," said Mr. Ford. "I'm not stopping until we get to Aunt Sue and Uncle Jack's house."

"Look at all this stuff," said Sharon to her brother, Steve. "You must have a ton of camping gear in here." She pointed at the bags and boxes piled high in the back of the van.

"I don't have any more stuff than you do," said Steve. He put on his tape player's earphones so he wouldn't have to listen to her.

"Now children, don't fight, said Mrs. Ford. "This is supposed to be a *vacation*."

They had been driving about two hours when all of a sudden there was a loud bang. The van slowed way down. Mr. Ford pulled off the road. He looked at his wife.

"What could be wrong?" she said.

"I don't know. I just had the van checked," her husband replied.

He got out of the van. He opened the hood and looked at the engine. "Oh no," he groaned. "A spark plug blew. We're not going anywhere until we can get a new one."

(continued)

"Dad," Sharon said, "didn't we get some spare plugs last time we went to the garage?"

"I forgot about that," her father said. "Guess what?" he groaned again. "The tools and spare parts are under all the stuff in the back."

Mrs. Ford gave her husband a long look. "Do you mean we have to unpack the whole van just to get one small spark plug?"

"I'm afraid we do. Come on, kids. Give me a hand," he said to Steve.

Mrs. Ford tapped her son on the shoulder. Steve kept listening to his tape player. "Steve," Mrs. Ford said in a loud voice.

"What's going on?" Steve asked his mother.

"Please help unload the van," his dad said. "We need to get the tools out of the back."

"Can't Sharon do it?" Steve asked.

"It's your ton of camping gear," said Sharon. "Come on."

"See if I let *you* use any of it," Steve said, getting out of the car.

"Children!" The parents said at the same time.

"Stop your fighting," said their father.

"We'll never get to your cousin's house if you stand here and fight," their mother added.

In about half an hour, the Fords were on their way again. This time the back wasn't quite so neatly packed. But the box of tools and spare parts was right on top—just in case of more bad surprises.

Story 5: Exercise

Circle the letter of the best answer.

1. **Main Idea:** This story tells about

    (a) the Ford family at the Olympics

    (b) the Fords visiting Aunt Sue and Uncle Jack

    (c) the Fords having trouble with their van

2. **Details:** The van stopped because

    (a) it was out of gas

    (b) it blew a spark plug

    (c) it had a flat tire

3. **Sequence:** After Sharon started to help her dad,

    (a) Mrs. Ford tapped Steve on the shoulder

    (b) Mrs. Ford got out of the van

    (c) Mrs. Ford started to cry

4. **Cause and Effect:** If Steve and Sharon stand and fight,

    (a) their parents will be angry

    (b) it will be lunch time

    (c) they will never get to their cousin's house

5. **Drawing Conclusions:** The tool box is on the top of all the Fords' stuff because

    (a) Mr. Ford couldn't find a place to put it

    (b) they're expecting to have a flat tire

    (c) they don't want to have to unpack all their stuff again

Unit 4

Time Words

Survival Vocabulary Stories

Story 1

Sandy wanted a watch for her birthday. For the past month, she had hinted and hinted that all she wanted was a watch.

Her mom kept asking her what kinds of new clothes she would like for her birthday.

Her dad kept asking her what new tapes or videos she would like.

Sandy had just about given up hoping for a watch.

She marked off the days and weeks on the calendar in her room. Finally her birthday came. She got up early in the morning. But she knew she would have to wait until that night to open her presents.

The day seemed to drag by. It took hours before it was noon. Then the minutes crept by until afternoon.

When Sandy got home from school, she saw a big box wrapped in birthday paper.

Oh well, she thought. Mom and Dad must have bought me a whole bunch of new clothes and put them in one box. I guess I'll have to wait until next year to get a watch.

She was a little sad as she went to her room to do homework.

After what seemed like forever, the clock on her radio showed that it was almost time for dinner.

Good, thought Sandy. Soon I'll get to open my present.

She went downstairs and asked her mom if she could help get dinner on the table. Her mom said that since it was her birthday, she didn't have to help. She could relax and watch the evening news on cable TV.

At last dinner was ready. Her mom and dad talked on and on. Sandy thought they had forgotten that it was her birthday.

(continued)

"Let's see," her dad said. "What's the date today?"

"Oh, Dad. You know what the date is. It's my *birthday*," Sandy said.

"How could I forget?" her dad grinned. "I guess it's time to open that present. What do you think?" He turned to Sandy's mom.

"I bet Sandy's been counting the seconds until she could open it."

Sandy picked up the big box. She set it on her lap. She could barely fit her arms around it. She shook it. She poked it. It didn't weigh much. It didn't make any noise.

She began to take the paper off. When she got the box open, she looked inside. There, she found another box. It was smaller than the first. She opened that one, too. Inside was another box.

"Hey," she said to her parents. "Is this some kind of joke?"

"Sort of," her dad replied.

Sandy kept opening boxes. She must have opened half a dozen. By the time she got to the last one, the box was quite small. She began to smile as she tore the paper off.

"You sure fooled me," she said. "I thought you had forgotten what I wanted."

She lifted the top of a small black velvet box. Inside was a digital watch just like the one she had been asking for. It had numbers instead of hands. When she pushed the side button once, the date showed up. When she pushed the button again, the face of the watch lighted up. In one corner it showed A.M. for morning or P.M. for evening.

"It's perfect! Thank you," she said. She hugged her mom and dad. "I bet the boxes were your idea, Dad."

"I'll never tell," he said, laughing. "Now let's have some birthday cake. All this waiting has made me hungry again."

Story 1: Exercise

Circle the letter of the best answer.

1. **Main Idea:** The best title for this story is

    (a) Sandy's Watch

    (b) The Birthday Surprise

    (c) Sandy's Birthday

2. **Details:** Sandy opened at least

    (a) three boxes

    (b) ten boxes

    (c) half a dozen boxes

3. **Sequence:** After Sandy got home from school,

    (a) she saw her birthday present

    (b) she did her homework

    (c) she had a snack

4. **Cause and Effect:** When Sandy saw a big box,

    (a) she thought her mom and dad had given her clothes

    (b) she thought it was a joke

    (c) she felt excited

5. **Drawing Conclusions:** After Sandy opened three of the boxes,

    (a) she threw the paper on the floor

    (b) she knew her parents had fooled her

    (c) she couldn't guess what her present was

6. **Activity:** Write about a birthday present you liked. Or write about a present you gave to someone else.

Story 2

Bzzzz! The green numbers on Don's digital clock said 6:30 A.M. "Ugh!" Don groaned as he remembered it was the first day of school. "It's too early in the morning. I'll never make it. Why don't they start school in the afternoon?" He rolled over and put the pillow over his head.

"Don! Time to get up!" his father called up the stairs.

Beep-beep-beep. The alarm on Don's digital watch went off.

"OK. I'm getting up." He pushed the button to shut off the alarm. Then he pushed another button to see the calendar. It said September 7. "I guess this really is the right date," Don muttered.

"Don! Are you coming?" This time his mother was calling him.

"In a minute," Don called back.

"You have less than an hour until the bus comes," his mother reminded him.

Don got dressed. He ate breakfast. Then, with about a second to spare, he ran out the door to catch the bus. On the bus, he talked to his friends about what they had done during the fast-passing weeks and months of summer. No one could believe that it was already the first day of school.

"It seems like just last week we were starting summer," Don said to his friend Najeeb.

"Yeah," Najeeb said. "I hope this school year zooms by as fast."

"I have a feeling that the hands of the clocks will creep by today," Don said. "I just hope I don't fall asleep."

"Look at my new watch," Najeeb said. "I'm all set in case classes are boring." He showed Don his watch. It had a small computer game built into it.

(continued)

"That's really neat," Don said. "My watch has an alarm. Maybe I'll set it so that it beeps just before the end of each class."

The bus pulled up outside the school. All the kids got off. Don and Najeeb found their first class. Before they knew it, it was noon—time for lunch. At lunch, they traded stories about their teachers. Both agreed that, so far, school had gone OK. Don had his gym class right after lunch. Then he had a study hall. The boys planned to meet on the front steps right after school.

Don's gym teacher made them run laps around the field. Then they had to do push-ups and sit-ups. Don found out that he wasn't in very good shape. He hadn't done this type of exercise during the summer. After gym class, he was tired. He was very glad to sit down in study hall. There were a lot of kids there. Don sat toward the back in a study booth. He set his watch alarm to beep just before the end of the period. Before long, he rested his head on his arms. I'll just rest for a minute or two, he thought. He began to think back over the day. In a few minutes, he had fallen asleep. The study hall teacher couldn't see him. No one bothered him.

With about five minutes left in the period, the teacher asked the students to be quiet so they could hear the afternoon announcements. Just as everyone quieted down, Don's alarm began to beep. It wasn't very loud, but he heard it. For a few seconds, he didn't know if it was morning or evening or *when* it was. Thinking that it was morning, he said in a loud voice, "OK. I'll get up now." The whole class burst out laughing.

Don looked around. His face turned very red.

"I think you had *better* get up," the teacher said. "You're going to have P.M. detention for sleeping in study hall."

"I guess I need to go to bed earlier at night," Don said. "I didn't mean to fall asleep. I'm sorry."

"Well, maybe I can overlook it this time," his teacher said. "OK, class, listen to the afternoon announcements." Don gave a big sigh of relief. He paid close attention for the last few minutes of class.

Name _____

Date _____

Story 2: Exercise

Fill in the blanks with the best answer.

1. **Main Idea:** This story is about a boy who

   _____

2. **Details:** Don's friend Najeeb had a watch with

   _____

   The gym teacher made the boys

   _____

3. **Sequence:** First, the alarm on Don's _____ went off.

   Then the _____ on his watch beeped.

4. **Cause and Effect:** After his gym class, Don was tired because

   _____

5. **Drawing Conclusions:** Don said, "OK. I'll get up now" because

   _____

Story 3

"Take a trip in the time machine! Step right up. Don't be shy." A man dressed in old-fashioned clothes called out to the crowd at the state fair. "We can take you to next month, next week, or next year. Buy your ticket now."

"What do you think?" Bonnie asked Gina. "I'd like to look ahead to the end of the school year."

"Not me," said Gina. "I'd like to go ahead exactly a hundred years. I want to know what people will be doing at this time on that very day."

"Let's try it," Bonnie said. She reached into her purse for fifty cents. She handed her money to the man.

Then she looked at her watch. The hands were both at noon. "I'd like to travel to the month of June," she said. "My friend would like to travel ahead one hundred years to this same date— the exact minute and second."

Gina nodded her head. She gave the man her money.

"This is a little unusual," the man said. "Two people in the time machine going to different times." He dropped their coins into a large carpenter's apron tied around his waist.

"So can we do it, or not?" Bonnie asked.

"We can try," the man said. "They don't call me Mr. Time Travel for nothing."

"I'm a little scared," Gina whispered to Bonnie. "I've read about people who get caught in a time warp and never come back."

"Those are just stories," Bonnie said.

"But I'm not sure I even believe in time travel," Gina said.

(continued)

62 *Survival Vocabulary Stories*

"You're not going to chicken out, are you?" Bonnie asked.

"Come on. There's nothing to worry about," Mr. Time Travel said.

"All right. I'm coming," Gina said. She took a last look at the sunny day, the crowd of people dressed in shorts and T-shirts, the cotton candy stand, and the Ferris wheel going around high above the fair.

Mr. Time Travel stepped between two faded blue curtains. He held the curtains open for the girls. They stepped through the opening.

There they saw a large, rusty metal container that looked like a huge tin can. On the outside were dials and buttons. The hands on several large clock faces showed the time at different places around the world.

A pile of calendars stood beside the giant tin can. Mr. Time Travel looked at one of the calendars. Then he turned some of the dials.

"That should do it," Mr. Time Travel said. He lifted a small flap of tin. "Climb in," he said, pointing to the inside of the can.

"Here goes," said Bonnie. "Do we have to do anything once we're inside?"

"No. Just sit still. Don't move at all. You could throw everything off balance. No telling where, or should I say when, you might end up."

At these words, Gina turned pale. "Just how does this work? I mean, how do you make us travel in this can thing?"

"If I told you that, then you'd want to build one of these yourself, now wouldn't you?" Mr. Time Travel said, smiling.

"Come on, Gina," Bonnie said from inside the can.

"OK," Gina said, taking a deep breath. She had barely stepped inside the can when Mr. Time Travel shut the flap. They could hear a key turning in a lock. "I don't think I like this," Gina said.

(continued)

"Look at how nice it is in here," Bonnie said. She tried to get Gina's mind off being scared. "Who would have guessed that it was so big inside. Such soft seats." She stroked the red velvet seats.

Suddenly the girls heard a loud, steady hum. The time machine began to shake. Gina sat down close to Bonnie. Their seats tipped back. The top of the can began to slide apart, right down the middle.

What they could see in the open space looked like the afternoon sky. The blue sky quickly turned to the colors of the evening sky. Then it turned pitch black like night. The set of colors began to repeat faster and faster.

"So, big deal," said Bonnie. "When do I get to the end of the year?" Just as she stopped talking, a summer scene flashed above them. People in bright-colored bathing suits played volleyball at the beach.

"For goodness sake. I wanted to see if I got any prizes at graduation," said Bonnie. "This is just a videotape of some people at a beach. I'm going to make him give us our money back." She tried to stand up. She lost her balance and fell back into her seat. The time machine rocked back and forth.

"Hey," she yelled. "What's happening?"

"Sit still," said Gina. Her voice sounded shaky. "He said not to move."

"Well, we may as well get our money's worth out of this dumb video," Bonnie said, settling back in her seat. More fast-changing sky colors followed the beach scene. "Your fifty cents worth must be coming on next," Bonnie said.

"Great," said Gina. "I just want to get out of here." Over their heads a scene showed robots with flashing lights moving in all directions.

"What are they doing?" Gina asked. "It looks kind of like the carnival, doesn't it? Don't tell me the state fair will look like that in a hundred years. No way!" she said. "There aren't any people. Wait, there are two people talking to one robot."

(continued)

"Well, I wouldn't pay much attention to this videotape," Bonnie said. "We sure wasted fifty cents on this." The loud hum began to die down. The sides of the can stopped shaking. "I should have known there was no such thing as time travel."

Bonnie looked at her watch in the dim light of the time machine. "Barely ten minutes have gone by."

"It seems like at least an hour. I'll be glad to get out of this so-called time machine," Gina said. "I don't care if it's AM. or P.M., as long as we're out on solid ground." The flap on the side of the can opened. The girls climbed out.

"I'm going to warn everyone who's waiting in line that this is a big fake," Bonnie said.

"Let's just get out of here," Gina said. "We're poorer but wiser."

They went back through the faded blue curtains. All of a sudden, Gina grabbed Bonnie's arm.

"What's that beeping and squeaking noise?" she asked. "It sounds like the robots we just saw in the time machine. We're not stuck ahead in time, are we?"

Bonnie laughed. "Don't be silly," she said. "It's just the noise of the Ferris wheel going around."

"Whew," said Gina. "For a minute there, I became a believer in time travel."

Story 3: Exercise

Fill in the blanks with the best answer.

1. **Main Idea:** A good title for this story is

_____

2. **Details:** Mr. Time Travel puts the money into a

_____

3. **Sequence:** First, the girls go to _____ , then they travel to

_____

4. **Cause and Effect:** Bonnie tries to stand up, which causes the time machine to

_____

5. **Drawing Conclusions:** Gina thinks they are stuck in the wrong time because

_____

6. **Activity:** If you could travel to any time, what would it be? Write about what you think life would be like in that time period.

Story 4

Mr. and Mrs. Brown watched the hands on the clock slowly travel from one number to the next. Seconds, minutes, and hours all ran together.

"How long have we been here?" asked Mrs. Brown, glancing at her watch.

"Only a couple of hours. But it seems like a day at least," Mr. Brown answered. Soft music played. Now and then a voice called over the loud-speaker for Dr. Nasser or Dr. Mendez or Dr. someone.

"Tell me again what happened," Mrs. Brown said. "I still can't picture it."

"It was just before noon," Mr. Brown began, "and I had finished the morning cleanup in the restaurant. We started to get lunch ready when the telephone rang. It was the wrong number."

"I know that part," Mrs. Brown broke in. "Get to the part about Billy."

"A few minutes later, a woman came running in the front door. She asked if we had a telephone. 'A kid on a bike has been hit by a car,' she said. 'We need to call an ambulance.' So I called for one. Then I went out front to see what I could do."

"And there you saw Billy," Mrs. Brown broke in again.

"Yes. There he lay. His leg was at a crazy angle. He was crying, of course. When he saw me, he calmed down a little. The best I can figure out, he came around the corner too fast and skidded in the sand. He fell into the path of the car. The car hit the bike. And Billy was thrown to the side of the road."

"Mr. and Mrs. Brown?" A woman in a white doctor's coat stood in front of them. "I'm Dr. Nasser."

"Yes. How's Billy?" asked Mrs. Brown.

(continued)

67

"Other then a broken leg and a few scrapes and bruises, he's doing fine. You can go in to see him now. Then I want to talk to you about his pills and the care of his leg."

"Oh, thank goodness," said Mrs. Brown. They followed the doctor down a long hallway into a small room with just one bed in it. Billy was lying very still. One of his legs was in a big, white cast. He opened his eyes and smiled weakly at his parents.

"He'll be a little groggy for a while," the doctor said. "By this evening, he should be able to eat dinner. But he needs to spend the night here. You can take him home tomorrow afternoon. He must stay in bed for a week. Then he can try getting up for a day and using crutches. After he has used crutches for a month, I want to see him again. He may be able to have a walking cast after that. It will be a year or so before his leg is as strong as it was. Do you have any questions so far?"

"I don't think so," Mrs. Brown said. "I wish I had a calendar to write down the different dates."

"Don't worry about that," said the doctor. "The nurse at the main desk will give you a list of dates, as well as a list of dos and don'ts."

"What about the pills you mentioned?" Mr. Brown asked.

"He takes one pill morning, noon, and night for the first few days for pain. After that, cut back to one pill in the A.M. and one in the P.M. After a week or so, he won't need the pain pills."

"Mom, Dad, I hope you're not mad," Billy said, his eyes still closed.

Mr. and Mrs. Brown looked at each other and then at Billy. "No, we're not mad," said Mr. Brown. "We're just glad you're still in one piece. You get some rest now. We'll talk later." Billy was asleep by the time his parents left the room.

Story 4: Exercise

Choose the best answer.

1. **Main Idea:** The best title for this story is

    (a) Billy Visits His Dad
    (b) Billy Breaks His Leg
    (c) The Bike Accident

2. **Details:** The accident happened

    (a) just after lunch
    (b) just before noon
    (c) in the afternoon

3. **Sequence:** A woman came running in the door, asking

    _____

    then Mr. Brown

    _____

4. **Cause and Effect:** Billy was riding his bike too fast around the corner, which made him

    _____

5. **Drawing Conclusions:** If Billy takes care of his leg, in one year

    _____

Survival Vocabulary Stories

Story 5

The clock said 6:00 A.M. Jane was already wide awake. She looked at the date on the calendar. Today was the day of the big race.

She had trained all year to get ready for this day. At 8:00 A.M., the starter would call all the runners to their marks. She would be joining five hundred other runners to begin the Cartersburg Marathon.

Before Jane had a chance to worry about the long day ahead of her, she jumped out of bed. She got dressed in her running clothes. She tied her hair back into a ponytail. She washed her face and hands. She brushed her teeth.

For breakfast she just drank some juice, because she didn't want to feel sick when she started to run. By 7:00 A.M., she was ready to go.

"Mom, let's go," she called up the stairs.

"Coming," her mom answered.

When her mom came downstairs, she helped Jane check everything to make sure she was ready. "You've got your watch?"

"Yes."

"How about your race number?"

"Yes."

"OK. I've got the water and this big timer clock. I'll set the hands at the right time when you start the race."

"Let's go," Jane said. "I don't want to be even a minute late. I'm getting nervous."

Her dad came in to wish her luck. "You'll do fine. Think about all the miles you've run this month," he said.

"Yeah, I know. I guess I'm ready. It's just that this last hour seems to take forever."

(continued)

"Just think, by this time this evening, you will have finished your first marathon," her dad said.

"I hope I finish this afternoon around 3:00 P.M. That would be really good time."

Jane and her mom drove through town. As they approached the starting point for the race, Jane's mom pulled into a parking garage. The crowd was so big she couldn't park any closer.

It was a beautiful morning, and the weather forecast was for a cool, clear day.

"It's a perfect day to run," Jane said.

"In my mind I'll be running every second with you," her mom said.

She gave Jane a big hug. "I'll meet you on the big hill at noon with some water and oranges."

"By that time, I'll be almost halfway to the finish line," Jane said, smiling.

She waved to her mom and disappeared into the crowd of people waiting for the starter's signal.

"Today is going to seem like a whole week to me," her mom said to herself. "I hope I can last until night." She felt tired just thinking about Jane running for six or seven hours.

A minute later, she heard the gun go off. She cheered as she saw Jane cross the starting line. Twenty-six long miles until Jane would finish her first marathon.

❖

Story 5: Exercise

Circle the letter of the best answer.

1. **Main Idea:** The best title for this story is

   (a) The Marathon

   (b) Jane's First Marathon

   (c) Jane Goes Jogging

2. **Details:** This was

   (a) Jane's first marathon

   (b) Jane's third marathon

   (c) Jane's tenth marathon

3. **Sequence:** Jane jumped out of bed. Then she

   (a) ate breakfast

   (b) got dressed

   (c) washed her face

4. **Cause and Effect:** If Jane eats breakfast, she might

   (a) not need to eat again

   (b) be late for the race

   (c) feel sick when she runs

5. **Drawing Conclusions:** Jane's mom felt tired because

   (a) she got up too early

   (b) she was thinking about Jane running

   (c) she didn't drink coffee at breakfast

6. **Activity:** Write about how you think Jane felt when she finished the marathon.

Unit 5

Food Store Words

Story 1

Carlos stood in front of the supermarket. People were pushing shopping carts full of groceries out the door marked "Exit." Baggers were helping by carrying out brown bags of food.

While he watched, Carlos thought about how much he wanted to work at the supermarket. He didn't want to be a cashier at the checkout counter. He was afraid he might not give the right change. He might get mixed up by all the store coupons and food stamps.

Instead, he would like to work in the deli. There, he could learn to slice meat and cheese. He decided to go in the door marked "Enter" and ask to see the store manager.

"May I speak to the manager?" he asked the clerk at the first checkout counter.

The clerk handed a receipt to a man. Then he turned to Carlos. "I think the manager is in the bakery department right now. That's down aisle six."

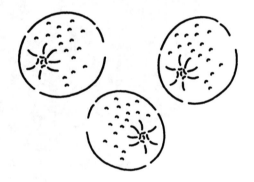

"Thank you," said Carlos. He walked past the produce department. He saw the green peppers. He smelled oranges and lemons. Then he walked down the aisle with all the frozen food. Brrrr. It's cold here, thought Carlos. Finally, he found the manager in the bakery department, talking to the bread man.

"Excuse me," said Carlos. "I would like to talk to you about working here."

"If you wait in the office," said the manager, smiling, "I will be with you as soon as I'm finished here."

"Yes. I will wait," said Carlos. He turned and walked back past the frozen food, past the produce department, and past the deli. When he found the office, he sat down to wait for the manager.

(continued)

"What did you say your name is?" asked the manager, as she walked into the office.

"My name is Carlos Montoya," said Carlos, standing up and shaking hands with the manager.

"Please sit down," said the manager. "What can I do for you?"

"I would like to work at this supermarket," Carlos replied. "Do you have any jobs in the deli department?"

"No, I'm sorry, we don't," said the manager. "But we need baggers and cashiers. Would you like one of those jobs?"

"I think I would like to be a bagger. Can you tell me more about it?" Carlos asked.

"Usually the baggers put groceries in brown bags at the checkout counter. Sometimes they help take a person's groceries to the car. They keep the baskets stacked up. They get the empty shopping carts from the parking lot and they keep them lined up. Sometimes the baggers stock shelves in the bakery or frozen food department. They also sweep the aisles. And they spray cool water on the fresh produce. Does this job interest you?"

"Yes," said Carlos. "I would like that job better than working as a cashier."

The manager smiled. She handed Carlos a form to fill out. "Why don't you fill out this form. Then you can tell me about any other jobs you have had."

"OK," said Carlos. He took a pen out of his pocket. He began to print neatly on the form. I hope I get this job, he thought.

Story 1: Exercise

Fill in the blanks with the best answer.

1. **Main Idea:** Carlos is going to try to get a job at the

   _____

2. **Details:** The store manager is in the _____
   department.

3. **Sequence:** Carlos walked past the produce department. Then he walked
   down the

   _____

4. **Cause and Effect:** If Carlos worked as a cashier, he might

   _____

5. **Drawing Conclusions:** If Carlos waits in the office,

   _____

6. **Title:** The best title for the story is

   (a) Carlos Goes Shopping

   (b) Looking for a Job

   (c) The Supermarket

Story 2

Mrs. Plant disliked going to the supermarket. "I spend all this money every week. Then I have to go and buy all the same food the next week."

Her kids were used to hearing her complain about shopping for groceries. When Saturday morning came around, they knew what to expect. Mr. Plant would try to help by saying that he could do the shopping. Mrs. Plant would shake her head and say, "No. I know what I need to buy. I'll just go and do it and get it over with."

One Saturday, Mrs. Plant decided to try a new store. She thought she might not mind shopping so much in a new place. She gathered up her coupons and drove off.

Right away, she liked the big shopping carts at the new store. And the clerks in each department seemed friendly.

Slowly she pushed her cart up and down the aisles. She kept checking her shopping list and crossing off items as she found them. In the deli, she found sliced corned beef. She didn't have that on her list. But she knew the kids would like it.

In the produce department, she saw a ripe, red watermelon which looked tasty. She crossed a few more items off her list in the frozen food department.

"I wonder if the kids would notice if I bought a new kind of frozen waffles," she mumbled. "The same old things, week in and week out. I could shop without a list, I bet."

"What's that?" An old man at the frozen food counter thought she was talking to him.

"Nothing. I was just talking to myself," said Mrs. Plant.

(continued)

She pushed her cart to the bakery department. There, she picked up hot dog rolls and three loaves of bread.

"Hmmmm. I like the looks of those coffee cakes. Maybe I'll buy one for Sunday breakfast." She popped it on top of the growing pile of groceries in her cart.

She picked up some fish for dinner. And she chose a small ham in the meat department. She had checked off everything on her list. She looked at her shopping cart piled high with food.

"Well, that ought to keep us eating for at least a week," she said. She looked at the big clock up by the checkout counter. Shopping in a new store had taken her twice the time she usually spent.

"Oh well. Coming to a new store was a *little* more fun." She started to unload her groceries. The cashier started scanning the prices coded.

While Mrs. Plant waited, the bagger carefully placed all her groceries in brown bags.

"My goodness. Six bags of food," said Mrs. Plant. "I hope I have enough money to pay for them." She gave the cashier her coupons.

"Do you have any food stamps?" the cashier asked.

Mrs. Plant shook her head no. The cashier said, "That will be one hundred and seven dollars, please."

Mrs. Plant counted out one hundred and ten dollars. She waited for her change and the receipt. The cashier handed her three dollars. Then he gave her a plastic number.

"What's this number for?" Mrs. Plant asked.

"We have a carryout service," the cashier explained. "Your bagged groceries are loaded in boxes. The boxes are sent out on a moving belt. You get your car, drive over, and give your number to the bagger waiting outside. The bagger matches your number with the number in the boxes and then loads the bags into your car."

(continued)

"That sounds good to me," Mrs. Plant said. "I think I like shopping at your store."

"Thanks," said the cashier. "Have a nice weekend."

Mrs. Plant took her number. She found her car in the parking lot.

"No heavy grocery bags to load," she said. "That helps."

She drove toward a sign that said "pickup" near the end of the store. She saw the bagger loading brown bags into a blue car. She handed the bagger her number as the blue car drove off.

He took the number over to the boxes of groceries on the ramp. He looked at the numbers on the boxes. He looked at the number in his hand. Then he looked at Mrs. Plant. He walked over to her car and leaned down to talk to her.

"Your number doesn't seem to match the number on any of the boxes."

"What? But that's the number the cashier gave me." Mrs. Plant got out of her car to look in the bags of groceries. "No. These aren't my groceries. I had corned beef and coffee cake and hot dogs and watermelon." She began to turn red.

"Uh-oh," said the boy. "I may have just put your groceries in that blue car. If you can just wait, they'll find the mistake when they get home. I'm sure they'll come right back."

"I'm certainly not going to wait for that to happen," said Mrs. Plant "They might live in the next town. It could be hours before they come back here. I demand to see the manager."

The manager hurried out to speak to Mrs. Plant. "I'm *so* sorry," he said. "Let me help you. We'll just go in and get you a new set of groceries."

"Oh," groaned Mrs. Plant. "Just when I almost thought shopping was fun, this had to happen. Now I have to shop *twice* for one week's food." Unhappily, she followed the manager back through the door marked "Enter."

Survival Vocabulary Stories

Story 2: Exercise

Fill in the blanks with the best answer.

1. **Main Idea:** A good title for this story is

   _____

2. **Details:** Mrs. Plant bought _____ in the deli.

3. **Sequence:** Mrs. Plant paid the cashier. Then the cashier gave her a

   _____

4. **Cause and Effect:** Mrs. Plant had to shop twice because

   _____

5. **Drawing Conclusions:** Do you think Mrs. Plant will want to shop at the new store again?

   _____

   Why?

   _____

Story 3

"Amy, will you go to the supermarket for me?" Mr. Chen asked. "I'm in the middle of my homework," Amy said.

"We need a few groceries before we can cook dinner," Mr. Chen said. "And I need to be at home in case your mother needs a ride home from work."

"All right," said Amy. "But I hope I don't have to take coupons. I never remember to use them. And sometimes the cashier gives me the wrong change." He handed Amy a list.

"No coupons today," her father said. "And don't worry too much about the change."

"These are the things we need: ham from the deli, fresh beans from the produce department, and bagels from the bakery."

Amy put on her coat. She put the shopping list in her pocket.

As she walked to the store, she hoped she would see one of her friends. She was almost to the store when she met her friend Phil.

"Hi, Phil!" she called.

"Hi, Amy!" he answered. "What are you doing?"

"I'm going to the store for my dad."

"I'm making a pie tonight. I need to buy a frozen pie shell," Phil said.

Together they walked through the door marked "Enter." Amy picked up a basket to put her groceries in. Phil didn't take one.

Slowly they walked up one aisle and down another. Near the deli, they saw the store manager telling a shopper where to find dog food.

(continued)

"What kind of pie are you making?" Amy asked Phil.

"Banana cream pie with lots of whipped cream," Phil said. "Oh. I guess I need to buy some bananas, too."

Amy laughed. "It's hard to make banana cream pie without bananas!"

Soon they had what they needed. They stood in line at the checkout counter.

Amy put her things on the counter first. The clerk scanned each item, then placed it in a brown bag.

"Do you have any coupons?" he asked Amy.

"No, not today," Amy answered. She gave the clerk the money for the groceries.

The clerk handed her the receipt. "There you go. You're all set."

Amy waited while Phil paid for his bananas and frozen pie shell. They walked out the door that had a big red "Exit" sign over it.

"See you tomorrow at school," said Amy. "Good luck with your pie."

"Thanks," said Phil. "If it's any good, I'll save you a piece."

Name _____

Date _____

Story 3: Exercise

Circle the letter of the best answer.

1. **Main Idea:** Amy and Phil were

    (a) on their way to school

    (b) baking pies

    (c) going to the supermarket

2. **Details:** Phil was making a

    (a) cake

    (b) banana cream pie

    (c) frozen pie

3. **Sequence:** Amy put on her coat. Then

    (a) she put on her hat

    (b) she said good-bye to her dad

    (c) she put the shopping list in her pocket

4. **Cause and Effect:** If Phil doesn't have any bananas, then

    (a) he can't make the banana cream pie

    (b) he will get sick

    (c) his mother will be mad at him

5. **Drawing Conclusions:** Amy doesn't like to go to the supermarket because

    (a) she always loses her list

    (b) she forgets to use her coupons

    (c) she doesn't like to shop

Story 4

"Good morning, all you folks out there in radio land. Today we find out who the lucky winner is in our Super Saver Supermarket Shopping Spree. Keep your dial set at 1900. In five short minutes, we'll make someone very happy. For now, more of our music to wake up to."

Music to wake up to, thought Randy. I don't want to wake up and go to school. But I guess I don't have much choice. I'll just listen to find out who the winner of the contest is. I can't remember if I entered that contest.

As he thought about it, the music lulled him back to sleep. All of a sudden, he woke up. Someone was saying his name.

". . . Randy Marks, you are our lucky winner. Just call me up. Then come right on down to the station. Pick up the ticket for your Super Saver Supermarket Shopping Spree. All the groceries you can fit into your shopping cart in five minutes. Randy Marks, if you're listening, today is your lucky day."

Randy jumped out of bed. He couldn't believe his ears. He called the station. He found out that what he had heard was true. He could pick up his winning ticket and go to the store anytime.

He ran downstairs to tell his mom and dad. After he told them, he asked them what he should try to buy during his five minutes.

"I'd spend a lot of time in the frozen food department," his mom said. "Think of all the ice cream and frozen pizza you could buy."

"Don't forget the bakery," his dad said. "But put the cookies and cakes on top of the frozen food. Otherwise they may get flattened."

(continued)

Survival Vocabulary Stories

"Are those departments close together?" Randy asked. "I don't have much time."

"Go in the door marked 'Enter.' On your right will be the deli. Just past the deli is the produce department. Grab some oranges and apples first. Pick up some fresh vegetables. Then count over three aisles. At the end by the checkout you'll find frozen foods. Go back one aisle to the bakery." His mother stopped to take a breath.

"Maybe I should do a practice run first. Then I'll know where everything is. Hey. I could skip school today to get ready."

"No you can't," his father said. "You'll have plenty of time after school. If you wait until 5:00, I'll come watch you after work."

"OK," Randy said. "But I don't see how I can sit still in school today." He finished his breakfast and ran for the bus stop.

School finally ended. Randy walked over to the radio station with a bunch of friends. He picked up his winning ticket. The station manager took Randy's picture for the local newspaper. Randy's friends clapped and cheered.

Then they all went to the supermarket. They went up and down all the aisles to see where everything was. Everyone had an idea about what Randy should pick up during his shopping spree.

At 5:00, Randy met the manager of the supermarket at the checkout counter. The manager said that when Randy was ready, the cashier would start the timer and Randy could begin.

"I guess I don't need to think about coupons or having the right change today, do I?" Randy joked.

"No, not today," the manager said. "Before you leave, we'll add up all your purchases and

(continued)

put them in brown bags for you. You'll get a receipt to show how much money your shopping spree has saved you. Are you all set to start?"

Randy saw his mom and dad come in the door. "I think I am," he said.

"Ready, set, *go!*" the manager said. The cashier started the timer. Randy took off running with his first shopping cart.

Five minutes later, he stood by the exit with three carts piled high with food. He smiled at his parents. He had filled one cart with frozen food, bakery products, and produce. He had filled the second cart with bags of potato chips. And he had filled the third cart with cases of soda.

"Randy, what are you planning to do with all those bags of chips?" his mom asked.

"And all that soda?" his dad added.

"I've invited all the kids in my class over for a party," Randy grinned. "Think I have enough food?"

His parents just groaned.

❖

Story 4: Exercise

Fill in the blanks with the best answer.

1. **Main Idea:** A good title for this story is

   _____

2. **Details:** Randy had his radio dial set at

   _____

3. **Sequence:** Randy ran downstairs to tell his mom and dad. Then

   _____

4. **Cause and Effect:** If Randy knows which aisles are next to each other,

   _____

5. **Drawing Conclusions:** At the end of the story, Randy's parents groaned because

   _____

Story 5

Mr. Mink always did his food shopping on Thursday. Early Thursday morning, he put on his big gray coat. It was rather long and baggy. He always took a big tote bag, which was empty except for some coupons.

On the way to market today, he stopped to pick up his four-year-old grandson, Ivan.

As always, the supermarket manager nodded as Mr. Mink came in with a shopping cart.

"Who's this?" the manager asked, smiling at Ivan.

"That's my grandson. Can you say hi, Ivan?"

Ivan shook his head. He hid behind his grandpa's long coat.

"You know how little ones are," Mr. Mink said. "He's shy. But he's going to be my helper today." The manager laughed. And Mr. Mink laughed.

He headed down the aisle toward the deli. "Here, Ivan," he said. "Hold my tote bag for me, please." Ivan did what he was told. He trailed along after his grandfather, dragging the big bag behind him.

Ivan got bored, waiting for his grandfather to buy ham and cheese at the deli. Ivan walked over to some big barrels full of candy. That candy looks good, he thought. I wonder if I could have just one piece.

He tried to get his grandpa's attention. But Mr. Mink was busy talking. Ivan meant to take just one. Somehow he ended up with a whole handful. He popped one piece in his mouth. He put the rest in the tote bag. I don't think Grandpa will mind, he said to himself.

(continued)

After the deli, Mr. Mink went to the produce department. He looked at every melon before he chose one. Ivan thought he would never make up his mind.

Ivan liked the looks of the shiny red apples and the bright yellow lemons. He put a few into the tote bag. I'm really helping Grandpa, he thought. He followed his grandpa into the bakery department.

"These rolls look good, Ivan, don't you think?" his grandpa asked. He put two boxes into the shopping cart.

Ivan had his eye on a chocolate cream pie. Yummy, he thought. As his grandpa went around the corner, Ivan picked up the pie and dropped it into the tote bag. The bag was getting kind of heavy. But he pulled it along behind him. And he tried not to bump into other people.

"The frozen food department is our last stop," his grandpa said. He picked out frozen beans and peas. Then he spent a long time deciding which frozen fish to buy.

Ivan wandered ahead to the big glass cases full of ice cream. He saw lots of boxes of frozen ice pops, like he saw on TV sometimes. Just then a shopper came along and opened the glass door. Ivan quickly reached in and grabbed two boxes. Into the bag they went. He also spotted some frozen waffles that looked awfully good. His grandpa came along just then. So Ivan skipped the waffles.

"OK. Let's head for the checkout counter," Grandpa said. Ivan nodded and walked along, dragging the tote bag behind him.

They stood in line for a long time. The cashier scanned all the groceries bought by the person ahead of them. Candy bars and gum were right at Ivan's nose level. He decided that he would try one of each kind. Into the bag they went. He was smelling the different kinds of bubble gum when his grandpa turned around.

"Put that back," Grandpa said. "No gum or sweets for you." He unloaded the shopping cart. The cashier scanned the groceries one by one. The clerk at the end of the counter put the groceries into brown bags.

(continued)

Survival Vocabulary Stories

"That's sixty-five dollars and five cents, please," said the cashier. "Do you have any coupons?"

"Yes," said Mr. Mink. "Ivan, please hand me my bag." Ivan held on tight to the bag. "Come on, give me the bag." Ivan pushed the bag toward him. It seemed awfully heavy.

Without paying much attention, Mr. Mink reached down into the bag for the coupons.

"What is *this*?" he howled. The manager rushed over. "Is anything wrong, Mr. Mink?" he asked. Mr. Mink pulled out a box of dripping ice pops. He dropped the box on the counter. Then he grabbed the tote bag.

"Yes. I mean no. I mean I don't know." He looked into the bag. One item at a time, he took everything out of the bag. He placed it all on the counter. When he was finished, there was a big pile of groceries. Mr. Mink didn't know what to say. Ivan didn't say anything, either.

"That's some helper you had today," said the manager. He started piling Ivan's groceries in an empty shopping cart. Those items would have to be put back on the shelves.

"I'm very sorry," Mr. Mink said. "I had no idea Ivan was such a helper." His face was quite red. He paid the cashier. The cashier gave him some change and a receipt.

"Hmmm," said the manager. "We'll have to be more careful next time, won't we?"

"I *was* being careful," Ivan said. He wondered why grandpa's face was so red. He smiled at the manager.

Mr. Mink took Ivan's hand and went straight toward the exit.

Story 5: Exercise

Fill in the blanks with the best answer.

1. **Main Idea:** This story is about a little boy who

   _____

2. **Details:** Mr. Mink wore

   _____

3. **Sequence:** First, Ivan put _____ in the tote bag. Then he

   _____

4. **Cause and Effect:** If Mr. Mink had paid more attention to Ivan, then

   _____

5. **Drawing Conclusions:** By the end of the shopping trip, the inside of the tote bag must have

   _____

Unit 6

School Words

Story 1

"Did you do your homework?" Hank asked. He and Vic were on the way to school.

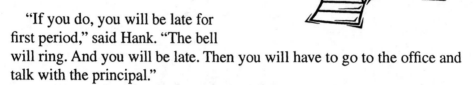

"Oh, *no*. I left my homework on my desk at home," said Vic. "I should run home to get it."

"If you do, you will be late for first period," said Hank. "The bell will ring. And you will be late. Then you will have to go to the office and talk with the principal."

"If I don't have my homework, the teacher will send me to the office anyway," said Vic. "Maybe if I say I'm sick, I can go see the nurse. Then I could be dismissed."

The boys walked a little farther. "If you get dismissed, you won't be able to go to gym. You will also miss mapping the microchips in computer class," Hank said.

"I like surfing the Internet best," said Vic. "It's almost as much fun as gym."

As the boys neared the school, they could see a long line of kids outside the cafeteria.

"Wonder what happened," Hank said. "Why is everyone standing outside?"

"Maybe there was a fire drill," Vic answered. "I wonder if we can go in the auditorium to wait."

The bell rang. The line of kids moved slowly inside. Hank could smell cookies baking in the cafeteria.

(continued)

"Sure smells good," he said to Vic.

"Sure does," Vic agreed. "I hope the class periods go by quickly before lunch. Maybe I won't go to the nurse to get dismissed. I don't want to miss gym *or* lunch."

The principal was standing outside the office.

"Good morning," he said to Hank and Vic.

"Good morning," Hank said. Vic mumbled something.

"Do you think he knows that I don't have my homework?" Vic asked.

"Don't be silly," Hank answered. "He doesn't know *everything*."

The boys got to their class. They sat down at their desks. The teacher said, "Take out your homework."

Vic took out a piece of paper and a pencil. He hoped the teacher would think it was his homework. Kids started calling out answers. The teacher wrote the answers on the board with chalk.

Vic kept his head bent over his paper. He couldn't wait for his next class. In the auditorium, the band began to play. The fire drill seemed like it had happened hours ago. The school day had started.

Story 1: Exercise

Circle the letter of the best answer.

1. **Main Idea:** This story is about a boy who

   (a) left his homework at home

   (b) left his lunch at home

   (c) left his lunch money at home

2. **Details:** Vic left his homework at home on his

   (a) kitchen table

   (b) desk

   (c) bed

3. **Sequence:** The bell rang. Then the boys

   (a) smelled smoke

   (b) saw a long line of kids

   (c) smelled cookies baking

4. **Cause and Effect:** If Vic goes home to get his homework,

   (a) he will be late for gym

   (b) his mother will be angry

   (c) he will be late for first period

5. **Drawing Conclusions:** Vic took out a piece of paper so that

   (a) the teacher would think it was his homework

   (b) he would have something to do

   (c) he could make a paper airplane

6. **Activity:** Tell what happens in your school if you forget your homework.

Story 2

Already it was the second week of school. The week would end with the big bonfire and pep rally. Jeff, the senior class president, called a class meeting in the auditorium after first period. The senior class always built the bonfire and planned the pep rally.

"OK. Quiet down," Jeff hollered. "We need to talk about the bonfire." The kids began to settle down and listen. "As you know it's coming up Friday night."

"First, we need someone to get a fire permit from the fire department."

Sally raised her hand. "I'll do that," she said.

"Thanks. Next someone has to talk to the principal and ask teachers to come and help that night."

Mr. Stern, the class adviser, raised his hand. "I'll take care of that," he said.

Just then, the loudspeaker came on. "All soccer players report to the gym."

"Uh-oh," said Jeff. "I have to go to that meeting. Meg, can you take over here?" He turned to Meg, the class vice president.

"I guess so," Meg said. "But I'm not sure what else we need to talk about."

"I can tell you," said Mr. Stern. "Here's a pencil and paper to pass around. The kids can sign up to help gather wood for the bonfire."

"OK. We need lots of help Friday after school," Meg said. "Meet in the cafeteria right after the bell. Does anyone have any questions?"

"I do." Mary raised her hand. "Let's do something different this year."

"Like what?" Meg asked.

(continued)

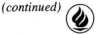

"Like get that old chicken coop from behind Mrs. Sims's house. We could drag it over to the field. Then Friday night, we could have a *big* blaze." The class started to cheer.

"Wow. That's a great idea," Meg said. She turned to Mr. Stern. "What do you think?"

"I'm not sure. Someone will have to ask Mrs. Sims if she wants to get rid of that chicken coop. Also, how would we get it here?"

Several kids offered to put it in the back of their pickup trucks.

Mary wasn't done. "We could put some old desks inside the coop. Then we could paint the name of the school we're playing on the outside."

"I get it," Meg said. "We're going to *burn* that team when we play them."

The class roared.

"We could stuff the chicken coop with newspaper," said Jason.

"Yeah," said Dave. "Then pour a little gas on the whole thing, and poof! We would have some bonfire!"

"Just a minute," said Mr. Stern. "Forget about the gas, or the whole thing's off. Mary, since this is your idea, why don't you ask Mrs. Sims about the coop. Then get back to me. I'll talk to the principal about it."

The bell rang. "Hold it a minute," said Meg. "If you signed up to help, be sure to be in the cafeteria Friday afternoon."

"We will," the kids all said at once.

"This is going to be the best bonfire ever," Meg said.

At lunch time, Mr. Stern went to the office to talk with the principal. Together they walked out to the field to look for the best place to have the pep rally.

(continued)

"I'm a little worried about this bonfire," Mr. Stern said.

"Me, too," the principal agreed. She drew a line with her foot. "I'll ask Coach Anton to make a chalk line here. Put pails full of water all around the chicken coop on this line. Don't let anyone get any closer to the fire," she said.

"I think I'll ask the nurse to come that night, just in case anybody gets hurt," Mr. Stern said.

"Everything will be fine, I'm sure," said the principal.

Friday afternoon came. Twenty kids were in the cafeteria waiting for Jeff and Meg to tell them what to do.

They all went out to the field. Some kids were dragging Mrs. Sims's chicken coop off a truck.

"Some of you can start filling the pails with water," Jeff said. "The rest of you can pile boards and papers inside the chicken coop."

"I've got a lot of old computer paper," said Jason. "I could fill this thing with that."

All the kids helped. Soon the chicken coop looked like a small one-room schoolhouse. They painted the name of the rival team's school on the side in big white letters. They painted "Burn Central High" on the other side.

By 4:00, everything was ready. Since the bonfire wasn't until 8:00, everyone went home.

No one was on the field at 6:00 to see someone splashing liquid from a red can inside the chicken coop.

(continued)

At 8:00, the school band started playing a spirited song. Soccer players ran onto the field, carrying torches to light the fire.

The first player tossed his torch into the chicken coop. There was a huge *bang*. Flames shot out of the doorway. The sides of the coop were pushed out, then pulled in. The flames started to roar. Bits and pieces of wood and paper flew out. Small fires started all over the field.

"Jeff, call the fire department," Mr. Stern yelled. "Meg, Jason, Dave. Quick! Dump these pails of water on the small fires. Oh dear. I was afraid something would go wrong."

The fire department came with sirens blaring. Soon the fire was under control. One soccer player had been hurt by a flying piece of wood. There were no other injuries. The cheerleaders tried a few cheers. But no one had much pep left for the rally.

Mr. Stern spoke to Jeff and Meg. "If you find out who put gasoline on this fire, let me know. That person can expect to have a long talk with the principal—and probably with the police, too."

Jeff and Meg looked glum. "The chicken coop was such a great idea," Meg said.

"Yeah. Too bad someone had to ruin it," Jeff replied.

Name _____

Date _____

Story 2: Exercise

Fill in the blanks with the best answer.

1. **Main Idea:** The seniors were having a class meeting to

   _____

2. **Details:** Mr. Stern said he would

   _____

3. **Sequence:** Just before the soccer players ran onto the field,

   _____

4. **Cause and Effect:** If someone puts gas on the fire,

   _____

5. **Drawing Conclusions:** Next year when the kids ask the principal if they can have a bonfire, she will probably say

   _____

6. **Activity:** Write about a pep rally or assembly you have had at your school.

   _____

Story 3

"This meeting is endless. When can we go home?" Dick asked Eva.

"Not until it's over. Let's go to the cafeteria and get some food. The teachers are selling cookies and punch," Eva said.

"When I said I would write up the town meeting story for the school paper, I had no idea I'd be here all night," Dick said.

Eva left her notebook on her chair. She and Dick walked out of the auditorium. "I hope there isn't a long line for food."

"Hi, Ms. Fry," Dick said to his computer science teacher as they walked into the cafeteria.

"Hi, Dick. Hi, Eva. Are you here for the school paper?" Ms. Fry asked.

"Yes," Dick answered. "Do you think they'll get to talking about the school budget tonight?" He picked up a cookie as he waited for Ms. Fry to answer. Eva moved to another table and poured herself some punch.

"I sure hope they do," said Ms. Fry. "I need to know if we have money to buy microchips to update computers, and new hardware and software. Also we need money to stay linked to the Internet."

"What about a new floor for the gym?" Dick asked. "Do you think the School Board put that in the budget?"

"I think it's in the budget. But the voters may not vote yes for it. Oh, excuse me," said Ms. Fry. "I need to go talk to the principal. See you tomorrow." She walked over to the other side of the room. The principal was there talking to some teachers.

"Hey, Eva," Dick called. "How about a fire drill? If I pull the fire alarm maybe everybody will go home now."

(continued)

"Yeah. But you'll have to spend a lot of time in the office tomorrow. The principal's office and the police office," Eva answered.

"Well, back to the meeting. We don't want to miss any big news stories," Dick said, putting some cookies into his pocket.

"If you eat all those cookies, you're going to need the school nurse," Eva said.

"I'll share them with you around midnight. We'll both need some energy then," Dick laughed.

They returned into the auditorium. Just then, a voter stood up and said, "I move to cut next year's school budget by two percent."

"We came back in at a good time," said Dick. "This meeting is going to move along now."

"Yes. But did you hear what he said? If they cut the budget, what will happen?" Eve asked. "What if they get rid of some of our sports teams?"

"That would be awful," Dick said. "Take good notes, so we can report this in the newspaper." They both wrote as fast as they could.

The voters talked on and on. Midnight arrived. Still not everything was decided.

Eva yawned. "I've got to go home and get some sleep. Do you have any of those cookies left?"

Dick smiled. "I told you these would come in handy around midnight."

"Well, they've made all the big cuts. What else is there?" Dick asked. "I think we can leave now. We've got *some* story to tell."

They stood up to leave. But another voter spoke. "I make a motion to freeze spending on all outside school activities."

(continued)

"All those in favor," said the chairperson. There was a loud "Aye" from the crowd. "Those opposed," . . . silence.

Dick and Eva looked at each other. "Oh *no*," they both groaned. "That means we won't have money for another issue of the school newspaper. We've been here all night for *nothing*," said Dick. "No one will ever hear our story about this meeting. I knew I should have pulled the fire alarm."

"This makes me so mad," said Eva. "Let's put out our *own* newspaper and pay for it ourselves."

"Great idea," said Dick. "I'll buy the computer paper. You can sign us up for two computers after school. Make sure they have the newsletter software on them," Eva said.

"See you tomorrow. Don't forget to bring some more cookies," Eva said.

They walked out of the auditorium, looking much less tired than they had a few minutes earlier.

Story 3: Exercise

Answer in complete sentences.

1. **Main Idea:** Why are Dick and Eva at this meeting?

   _____

   _____

2. **Details:** Which teacher do Dick and Eva talk to?

   _____

   _____

3. **Sequence:** Ms. Fry talked to Eva and Dick. Then she

   _____

   _____

4. **Cause and Effect:** Why won't there be another issue of the school newspaper?

   _____

   _____

5. **Drawing Conclusions:** Why do you think Dick and Eve were feeling a little less tired when they left the meeting?

   _____

   _____

Story 4

Everyone was watching the clock. It was last period on Friday. Teachers cleaned up their desks. They wiped chalk off the board. Kids put away their pencils and paper. They put their homework in their backpacks. The bell rang. Class was dismissed for the week.

"Hey, Tasha, are you going to help get ready for the dance?" Pete asked. "This is going to be the best dance of the year. And the money from the tickets should really help the school buy more computers."

"Yes," Tasha said. "I have to stop in the office first. The principal wants to talk about using that money for new computers. I'll meet you in the auditorium."

"I will be in the cafeteria, not the auditorium. We have to move all the big tables out," Pete said.

"Oh no. That will be a big pain," Tasha said. "I'll get there as soon as I can." She put her books in her locker and banged the door shut.

Pete saw some other kids from his class. He went to ask them to help. Soon a large group started folding up the tables. They carried the tables out of the cafeteria, down the hall, and into the gym. Mr. Gray, the teacher in charge, also helped. Tasha got there just as the last table was moved.

"Sorry I missed helping," she said to Pete.

"Don't worry. Tomorrow night after the dance, we have to move all the tables back. You can help then," Pete smiled. "OK, everybody. Be back here tomorrow at noon. And don't forget to bring your decorations. We'll transform this place into Technology Heaven. No one will know this is really a cafeteria." The kids laughed as they looked around the cafeteria.

"I still think I'll know it's where I stand in line for lunch," Andy said.

(continued)

"Yeah, and have food fights," Gene added.

"No," said Pete. "By tomorrow night, it will look like Computerland."

Saturday noon, all the kids met at school. Mr. Gray unlocked the door to the cafeteria. Some of the kids brought in cartons full of computer disks. Others had databases and spreadsheets taped together. There was one very long strip of computer graphics printouts.

Andy came in late. He had printed some enlargements of microchips.

"Where were you?" Tasha asked.

"I almost didn't come," Andy said. "My date just called to tell me she can't go tonight."

"How come?" Pete asked

"She's sick," Andy answered. "What a bummer. I was looking forward to this dance."

"That's too bad," Tasha said from the top of a tall ladder. She was hanging floppy disks from the ceiling.

"Oh well. That's life," Andy said. "What can I do to help?"

"Let's pass these disks up to Tasha to hang," Pete suggested.

Once, the boys shook the ladder. Tasha screamed.

Mr. Gray didn't think it was funny. "The school nurse isn't here today. Let's not have any broken bones."

Pete and Andy said they were sorry. They went to get small tables from the library. They made a place for kids to sit between dances. Mr. Gray made them move a table that was in front of the exit door.

"We can't block an exit in case of fire," he explained.

For tablecloths, Tasha put down a database or spreadsheet on each table. Other kids hung up the microchip prints. By 4:00, the kids agreed that it didn't look like the cafeteria any more.

(continued)

"It looks great," said Pete. "But how do I get on the Internet?" The kids laughed.

"You all did a good job," Mr. Gray said. "Tasha, you worked extra hard."

"Thanks, Mr. Gray. I can't wait until tonight," she said. "I've got to go now. I see my dad outside."

"Bye," Pete said. "See you tonight."

Tasha got in the car. "Boy, am I tired," she said. "My arms are killing me. I had to reach up over my head to hang disks. It's OK though. The cafeteria looks like a new place." She stopped talking and looked at her dad.

"Tasha, I have some bad news," her dad said.

"What?" Tasha asked.

"Your date for tonight called. He's really sick."

"Oh no," said Tasha. "After all my hard work. It's not fair."

Her dad started to drive away from the school.

"Wait. I have an idea," Tasha said. "Stop the car." Her dad stopped. Tasha jumped out of the car. She ran over to Andy's car. He rolled his window down.

"Guess what," she said. "You have a date for tonight after all."

"I do?" he said.

"Yeah, me. My date got sick, too."

"Hey, that's great! I mean that's too bad. Whatever! I'll pick you up at 8:00," Andy smiled.

"I'll be ready," Tasha laughed. "We don't want to miss the dance, after all our hard work."

Story 4: Exercise

Circle the letter of the best answer.

1. **Main Idea:** The best title for this story is

   (a) The Dance

   (b) Getting Ready for the Dance

   (c) At the Dance

2. **Details:** Tasha couldn't help after school because

   (a) she had to see the nurse

   (b) she had to talk to her boyfriend

   (c) she had to see the principal

3. **Sequence:** After the boys shook the ladder,

   (a) Tasha screamed

   (b) Tasha fell off

   (c) Tasha got off the ladder

4. **Cause and Effect:** Tasha's arms hurt because

   (a) she had been swimming

   (b) she had moved too many tables

   (c) she had been reaching up to hang computer disks

5. **Drawing Conclusions:** Tasha and Andy didn't want to miss the dance because

   (a) they like to dance

   (b) they had both worked hard decorating the cafeteria

   (c) their friends would be there

Story 5

Mrs. Card drove, and Simon sat in the front seat.

"But I don't *want* to move," Simon said.

"We don't have a choice," his mother said. She patted Simon on the back. "I can't pass up this new job. I'm sure you'll like school in Maine."

"No, I won't. I won't have any friends. How can you *do* this to me?" Simon looked out the car window. Brown smog was rolling over the city. He thought about going to school in the country. He could feel the tears coming.

"One reason we're driving up to Maine today is so you can see your new school. We'll meet the principal. And you can have a chance to go to some classes."

"Is that supposed to make me *happy* or something?" Simon asked. "I *refuse* to like it."

"I'm sorry you feel that way, Simon dear. I'm doing my best to help you get off to a good start."

They rode the rest of the way without talking. After many hours, they drove into a small town. The streets had tall trees. The houses were all painted white. In the middle of the town was a big park with green grass.

"I'll stop at a gas station to ask the way to the school," Mrs. Card said.

"I can't *believe* this," Simon said. "There isn't even a fast-food place anywhere."

"Oh, look. I don't even need to ask the way. There's the school." Mrs. Card pointed to a large brick building. A black metal fire escape zigzagged down one side of the building.

(continued)

"Looks like they have to have a lot of fire drills there," Simon said.

"I'll bet they don't even have an auditorium." He sank lower in his seat. His mom pulled into a parking space.

"Come on," his mom said. "We'll find the office first." She walked quickly toward the front steps. Simon followed slowly behind.

Just as they reached the front door, the bell rang. The period was over. Kids filled the hall. Simon heard some kids talking about microchips and the Internet.

A voice came over the loudspeaker, calling kids to the computer lab. A teacher with chalk dust all over his hands walked by. He smiled at Simon and said, "Hi." Kids stood in line at the school store. They were buying paper and pencils.

"So far this is a lot like school back home." Simon sounded surprised. He took a deep breath. "Let's go to the office."

The principal welcomed them into her office. She sat at her desk and Simon and his mom sat on a soft couch. They all talked for a while. The principal told Simon what time school started in the morning and what time it was dismissed. She asked Simon if he had any questions.

"Just one," said Simon. "Do you have an auditorium? I like to act in school plays."

"We have a stage in the gym and one in the cafeteria," the principal said. "I think you'll like our drama program. We have two plays and a musical each year. Do you like to sing?"

"Yes," Simon said. "I'm in the chorus. But I really like acting best."

"Why don't I find a student to show you around the school? Then you can see some classes." The principal stood up. She asked the secretary to find a student in study hall who could show Simon around.

(continued)

In a few minutes, a boy Simon's age entered the office. "Hi. I'm Kurt," he said.

"This is Simon," said the principal. "Will you take him around school?"

"Sure," Kurt answered. "Come on, Simon. Tell me where you're from . . . ."

In a few minutes, the boys were talking like old friends.

"Well," said Mrs. Card to the principal. "Maybe Simon isn't going to hate this after all."

The principal smiled. "You've had quite a day. Why don't we go have some coffee while we wait for the boys to come back. Aren't teenagers fun?" The two women laughed.

Story 5: Exercise

Fill in the blanks with the best answer.

1. **Main Idea:** This story is about

   _____

   _____

2. **Details:** There is a _____ on the outside
   of the school building.

3. **Sequence:** After Simon talked with the principal, Kurt

   _____

4. **Cause and Effect:** Simon had to move because

   _____

   _____

5. **Drawing Conclusions:** How do you think Simon will like his new school?

   _____

   _____

   _____

   Why? _____

6. **Title:** A good title for the story is

   _____

Unit 7

Health Words

115

Story 1

Justine was visiting her Aunt Pat and Uncle Mike. They had a summer house on a big lake. All week, Justine watched her cousins water-ski. She wanted to try it, too. On Saturday, her mom and dad came to pick her up.

"We can't go home until I try to water-ski," Justine said.

"Right," said Uncle Mike. "You can't leave without at least trying it."

"I'll get the boys to drive the boat," said Aunt Pat. Justine's mom and dad sat on the beach and watched.

The boys brought the boat close to shore. Justine put on a life jacket and swam out to the boat.

She put her feet in the skis. She had a hard time keeping the tips up. The skis flopped this way and that.

The boys steered the boat away from the shore. The boat went faster and faster. The rope between Justine and the boat grew tight.

For a few seconds, she stood up on the skis. Then she fell over. She let go of the rope and floated in the water. The boat came back to pick her up. She tried again. No luck.

Uncle Mike called out some suggestions. Aunt Pat swam out to talk to Justine. Justine tried again. Each time she stood up for a few seconds then fell. "One more try," she called to the boys in the boat. They circled back near her. This time she took a long time getting ready.

"OK," she called. The boat started up and pulled away fast. Justine fell over again. This time she didn't pop back up again. She hadn't let go of the rope. The boat was dragging her through the water.

(continued)

"Help! Help!" she screamed. She was being dragged under the water. The grown-ups were all shouting "Stop" to the boys in the boat. Finally, the boat stopped.

Justine's dad had already jumped into a canoe. He almost tipped it over. He paddled way to the right then way to the left of where Justine was.

Meanwhile, Aunt Pat swam out to Justine. She pulled her in to shore. Justine was crying and holding her arm.

"It hurts. It hurts," she said over and over.

"I'll get an ice pack," said Uncle Mike.

"What happened?" Justine's mom asked.

"I got the rope caught around my arm," Justine sobbed. "I couldn't let go. The more the boat pulled me, the tighter the rope got." She burst into tears again.

"Oh dear," said Justine's mom. "I think we'd better call the hospital and take her to the emergency room. Her arm may be broken."

"First let's clean the scraped part with antiseptic. Then we can put ice on it," Aunt Pat said.

"It's so sore," cried Justine. "I don't want anyone to touch it."

"Now, dear. We have to see how badly you're hurt," Justine's mom said. "I'll help you get into some dry clothes. Then we'll do what Aunt Pat and Uncle Mike suggested."

They went into the house. Justine was shivering. Her lips were turning blue.

"I think you're in shock," said her mom. "Do you feel sick to your stomach?"

"No, I just ache all over," Justine answered. Her mom helped her get dressed. She was careful not to touch the sore arm. She fixed a sling out of a big bandage.

(continued)

Justine drank some hot cocoa. She said she felt better. Her arm had white marks on it where the rope had pulled tight. Her upper arm had deep rope-sized dents all around.

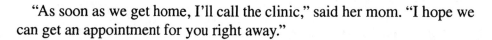

"I don't think it's broken," her mom said.

"Maybe it's a bad sprain," Aunt Pat suggested.

"It's a bad *something*," said Justine.

"As soon as we get home, I'll call the clinic," said her mom. "I hope we can get an appointment for you right away."

"I think the doctor will take a good look at it. Then he'll have the nurse X-ray it. You will probably have to keep ice on it for twenty-four hours," said Uncle Mike. "Then, use a heating pad. You'll be healthy again before you know it."

"I think I might wait a while before I try waterskiing again," Justine said.

"I agree with that," her dad said. "I got a few new gray hairs today."

"You need to have some lessons in paddling the canoe," Justine laughed.

"I guess I did look pretty foolish," her dad said, joining in the laughter. "Anyway, you're safe. That's what counts." He hugged Justine, being careful not to touch her sore arm.

Story 1: Exercise

Circle the letter of the best answer.

1. **Main Idea:** This story is about a girl who

   (a) knew how to swim

   (b) hurt her arm waterskiing

   (c) knew how to paddle a canoe

2. **Details:** Justine had a hard time

   (a) keeping the tips of the skis up

   (b) driving the boat

   (c) paddling the canoe

3. **Sequence:** After she stood up for a few seconds,

   (a) she zoomed over the water

   (b) she floated

   (c) she fell

4. **Cause and Effect:** As the boat went faster,

   (a) the rope pulled tighter

   (b) Justine skied better

   (c) the boys screamed

5. **Drawing Conclusions:** Justine's dad got more gray hairs because

   (a) he is old

   (b) he was scared Justine was drowning

   (c) he thought he would fall out of the canoe

Story 2

Brad had to go to the dentist. It was his six-month appointment. He didn't mind going, because he had never had a cavity. He even told his little sister that going to the dentist was fun. She didn't believe him.

Before going to his appointment, Brad brushed his teeth. Then he gargled with some mouthwash. I'm glad I have such healthy teeth, he thought. He smiled at himself in the mirror.

He sang as he got into the car and started off for the dentist's office. Halfway there, he had to pull over because an ambulance zoomed up behind him. Its lights were flashing, and its siren was on full blast. There must be some emergency, he thought.

Brad waited a short time in the waiting room, reading magazines.

Dr. Jarvis, the dentist, asked Brad if his gums hurt or if he had any toothaches. Brad said no, and kept smiling.

After his teeth were cleaned, Brad rinsed his mouth with antiseptic mouthwash. Then he sat back in the chair. Dr. Jarvis told him that his teeth looked fine. Brad just smiled.

"Now, we'll do some X-rays to see how your wisdom teeth are doing," the dentist said.

"Wisdom teeth?" asked Brad. "What are they?"

"They're the last teeth you get," Dr. Jarvis said. "Usually we have to pull them out."

"But why?" Brad asked.

"Because there's no place for them to fit in your mouth," the dentist answered.

(continued)

"Open wide," said Dr. Jarvis. She placed a piece of cardboard in Brad's mouth. "Now bite down hard and don't move," she said. Then she left the room. The X-ray machine buzzed.

"Now the other side, and you're all done." She put cardboard X-ray film into the other side of Brad's mouth.

"Now what?" Brad asked when it was all done.

"Just wait a few minutes and we'll read the X-rays." Dr. Jarvis left the room again. Brad daydreamed in the chair. His gums were a little sore where the cardboard X-ray had rubbed.

"Well," said the dentist, "your wisdom teeth have to come out."

Brad groaned. "When, now? Do I have to go to the hospital?" he asked.

"No. We'll give you another appointment. Then we'll take them out right here in the clinic," his dentist said. "Dr. Sanjay is an oral surgeon. He's the doctor who does all our wisdom teeth."

"It's going to hurt a lot, isn't it?" Brad asked.

"Well, let's put it this way. It may hurt more than a sprained ankle. But it won't hurt as much as a *broken* ankle. Some people have very little pain. We'll give you some medicine for the pain, just in case. For forty-eight hours you keep an ice pack on your face. After that, you use a heating pad until the swelling goes down."

"This sounds awful," Brad said. "It will be worse than being sick." He thought he would look like a cartoon character with a bandage around his jaws. His cheeks would be all puffed out. He didn't hear what the dentist was saying to him.

"What?" he asked.

"I said, just have your mom call for an appointment." The dentist left the room. Slowly, Brad left, too. He wasn't smiling any more.

"So how was it?" his sister asked when he got home. "Fun?"

Story 2: Exercise

Fill in the blanks with the best answer.

1. **Main Idea:** This story is about

   _____

   _____

2. **Details:** Brad will have to have his _____
   taken out.

3. **Sequence:** Before he left home, Brad

   _____

   Next, he gargled with

   _____

4. **Cause and Effect:** Brad will have to have his wisdom teeth out because

   _____

5. **Drawing Conclusions:** After his visit to the dentist, Brad's smile was
   gone, because

   _____

Story 3

Max came home from school Friday with a headache and a sore throat.

His mother gasped when she saw him. "You look as white as a sheet," Mrs. Gold said. "What's the matter, Max?"

"I don't feel very well," Max said. "I think I'm getting a cold. My throat hurts."

"Go lie down in your room. I'll check to see if you have a fever. If you do, I think I'll call the doctor for an appointment," his mom said.

"I don't think I'm *that* sick" said Max. "I just need to gargle with salt-water. Besides, I want to go to the dance at school tonight."

"We'll see about that," his mom said.

Max lay down on his bed. He turned on his tape player. He closed his eyes. In a little while, his mom checked his temperature. It was 101.

"You're not going *anywhere* tonight," his mom said. She covered him up with a blue-and-white quilt. "Let me look at your throat."

She shined a flashlight into Max's throat. "I don't like the looks of that throat," she said. "There are white spots on your tonsils."

Max groaned. "Just let me sleep a while. I'll be all right."

"Drink this grape juice. I'm calling the clinic for an appointment." His mom left the room.

Max drank the juice. Then he sank back on his pillow. The rock stars on the posters on his wall seemed to be moving back and forth. Max shook his head a little, trying to clear his eyes. The rock stars swayed even more.

"I *must* be sick," Max muttered. Soon he fell asleep. He tossed and turned.

(continued)

About dinnertime, he woke up. He ached all over. His mom brought him some warm broth. She looked worried. When he closed his eyes, he felt like he was spinning around. His fever had gone up another degree, to 102.

"I feel so hot. Did someone put a heating pad in my bed?" Max asked.

"No, dear. It's your fever that makes you feel that way."

"Yeah. But in a few minutes, I'll feel like there's an ice pack in my bed. I'm so cold."

"Try to sleep some more," his mom said, turning out the light.

About midnight, she heard Max talking. She got up and went to his room. He was tossing and turning again. This time, he kept muttering about dancing. He seemed to be talking to the people on the posters in his room.

His mom put her hand on his forehead. He was burning hot. He didn't seem to know her.

She quickly went to the telephone and called the emergency number. In a few minutes an ambulance arrived at the house.

Two men in white coats carried Max to the ambulance. They let Max's mom ride in the back with him. He was still talking nonsense.

The emergency room doctor met them at the hospital. He checked Max. He shook his head when he saw how high Max's fever was. The lab technician came in and did some tests.

"What is it, Dr. Berry?" Mrs. Gold asked. "Max said he thought he was coming down with a cold."

"I'm afraid it's more than a cold," Dr. Berry replied. "Those tonsils need to come out. First, we need to bring down his fever. I'll start him on some medicine to get the illness under control. Then we'll operate."

(continued)

"Oh dear," said Mrs. Gold. "Max has never had anything worse than a sprain. I don't think he's going to like this."

"Well, this isn't something we can just bandage up," said Dr. Berry. "He'll feel better in the morning. And so will you. You go on home and get some sleep. Max will be well taken care of here."

Mrs. Gold looked upset. "I don't have a car to drive home. I came in the ambulance with Max."

"Oh," said Dr. Berry. "Well, why don't you spend the rest of the night here? We can put a cot in Max's room. Would that make you feel better?"

Mrs. Gold smiled. "That would be nice. Then I can be here when Max wakes up. He won't know what has happened or why he's at the hospital."

"I'll let the nurses know," said the doctor. "You can go on up to Max's room."

"Thank you, Dr. Berry. I feel better already."

Story 3: Exercise

Circle the letter of the best answer.

1. **Main Idea:** This story is about

    (a) a boy who has a cold

    (b) a boy who has a sudden bad illness

    (c) a boy who has the chicken pox

2. **Details:** Max's mother covered him with

    (a) a sheet

    (b) a bedspread

    (c) a quilt

3. **Sequence:** First, Max felt too hot. Then

    (a) he felt too cold

    (b) he felt better

    (c) he felt dizzy

4. **Cause and Effect:** Mrs. Gold called the emergency number because

    (a) she didn't know the doctor's number

    (b) Max's fever was much worse

    (c) she wanted to talk to someone about Max's illness

5. **Drawing Conclusions:** Max will miss quite a few days of school because

    (a) he's going to have an operation

    (b) he needs to get over his cold

    (c) his mother won't let him go to school while he's sick

6. **Activity:** Write a story about a time when you were sick.

Story 4

Hugo went to a meeting for students who wanted to help at the local hospital. Mr. Land, from the hospital, talked to the students for about one hour. He told them about some of the jobs they could do. He said they could work in the hospital or in the clinic. At the end of the meeting, he wrote down a list of their names and telephone numbers.

"I'll call you in a few days," Mr. Land said. "If you still think you'd like to help, we'll make an appointment for you to come visit the hospital."

Hugo went home and told his family at dinner about the meeting. "I think I'd like to be a doctor," Hugo said. "I can't wait for Mr. Land to call me. This will really be fun."

"It may be hard work, too," his dad said. "But I think it will be a good chance to see if you like working with sick people."

"Gag me," said his sister. "Who wants to be with *sick* people all day?"

"I like the idea of helping other people," Hugo said.

"Take your vitamin, dear," his mom said, "so you stay healthy."

"Do we have to start calling you Doctor?" his sister asked.

"You can call me anything you like," said Hugo as he left the table.

On Wednesday, Mr. Land called Hugo. They planned a time for Hugo to visit on Friday after school.

Hugo got to the hospital early. He waited for Mr. Land near the entrance to the emergency room.

Hugo had only been there a few minutes when an ambulance came zooming up. Some people had been badly hurt in a car accident.

(continued)

Hugo felt a little sick when he saw blood on the people's faces. He looked away. He hoped Mr. Land would come soon.

Next, a coach from the high school came in with a player who had been hurt in basketball practice. The girl had an ice pack on her arm. Hugo asked her what had happened.

"I fell on my arm and twisted it. Coach thinks it's a sprain. I have to have an X ray to make sure it isn't broken. What are you doing here?" she asked Hugo.

"I'm going to learn about being a volunteer. You know, to help around the hospital."

"That's not for me," the girl said. "This place gives me the creeps. See you later." She walked off to the X-ray department.

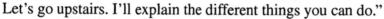

"Ah, here you are," said Mr. Land. "Sorry I'm late. Let's go upstairs. I'll explain the different things you can do."

"OK," said Hugo. "I can't wait to start."

"Here on the first floor is the gift shop. People like to buy cards for their friends who are sick. Sometimes volunteers help in here."

"I think I'd like to spend time with the sick people," Hugo said.

"The room for helpers is at the end of this hall," Mr. Land said. "A nurse tells you what to take to a sick person's room. Then you put things on a cart and push it down the hall," Mr. Land said.

"You don't give any medicine. Only nurses do that. And you don't do any blood tests. Lab technicians do that. But the nurse might tell you to take a heating pad to someone who has a back that aches. Or you might take a gargle to someone with a sore throat."

(continued)

"That sounds more like what I want to do," Hugo said.

"You can also help the nurses by folding bandages and keeping the supply room neat. At the end of the day, everything in the room needs to be cleaned with an antiseptic spray. So, does this sound like something you want to do?"

"Yes, it does. I'd like to work every afternoon after school."

Mr. Land smiled. "Why don't you plan to work two days a week to start," he said. "Then if you can get all your homework done and you want to work more days, you can. Can you start Monday?"

"I think I have a dentist appointment on Monday," Hugo said with a frown. "How about Tuesday?"

"That will be fine. Let's go down and fill out some forms. Then you'll be all ready to start on Tuesday," Mr. Land said.

The two walked down the hall. I think I'm going to like working here, Hugo thought. His sneakers made a squeaky sound on the shiny floor.

Story 4: Exercise

Fill in the blank with the best answer.

1. **Main Idea:** This story is about a boy who

_____

2. **Details:** The girl in the emergency room had hurt her

_____

3. **Sequence:** First, Hugo went to a meeting. Next, he got a

_____

from Mr. Land. Finally, he went to visit the

_____

4. **Cause and Effect:** Seeing the people in the ambulance made Hugo feel

_____

5. **Drawing Conclusions:** Hugo might be a good doctor because

_____

Story 5

Wanda More was a doctor. She had just finished medical school. All summer she worked in a clinic in New York City.

A lot of teenagers came to the clinic. Some of them were healthy. They just wanted a chance to talk to someone about their problems. Some of them had sisters who were taking drugs. Some had brothers who had been in fights. Some wanted to talk about becoming a lab technician or a midwife or a doctor, themselves.

The kids called her Dr. Wanda. She always listened to their problems. She wished she could help them more.

Once a week, Dr. Wanda went to visit the people who were too sick to come to the clinic. She took a black bag full of medicine with her.

When she got to an apartment building, she saw a lot of people—not just the person she went to see. She saw babies with sore throats. She saw old people with aches and pains.

Sometimes she gave people vitamins, bandages, and antiseptic creams. She had some good-tasting gargle that kids liked a lot.

She asked people to make an appointment at the clinic. That way she could check on them again. Sometimes she called a lab technician to take samples. Sometimes she called a dentist to come fix a bad tooth. Sometimes she called a midwife to help a mother give birth.

It seemed there were so many people needing attention that she could never take care of all of them.

One day, Dr. Wanda visited Mr. Lopez in his apartment. She was afraid the old man was getting sicker.

(continued)

         Survival Vocabulary Stories

It was cold. Some of Mr. Lopez's windows were broken, letting cold air blow in. When he didn't pay his rent, the landlord shut off the heat.

"Mr. Lopez, you need to go to the hospital for a while," she said.

"Too much money," was all Mr. Lopez kept saying. But he smiled at her.

Dr. Wanda tried to cover the broken windows with newspapers. She made some hot soup for Mr. Lopez. Then she called his landlord about some heat.

While she was there, a fight started out in the hallway. At first she didn't think much about it. Lots of times there were fights in these apartments.

But the angry voices got louder and louder. They were right outside Mr. Lopez's door.

"I'd better go see about that fight," Dr. Wanda said.

"Don't bother. It's just wild kids." Mr. Lopez shook his head sadly.

"This used to be a nice place to live. Before drugs made people crazy." He gave a sign and closed his eyes.

In the next apartment Dr. Wanda could hear a baby screaming.

All at once, the door to Mr. Lopez's apartment flew open. A man and woman fell into the room. The woman had a knife. She was slashing at the man.

"Stop that," Dr. Wanda shouted. She threw herself at the woman. The woman was so surprised that she dropped the knife. Dr. Wanda tried to hold the woman by the arm. But she broke away from her. She ran out the door, yelling loudly.

The man lay bleeding on the floor. He had several stab wounds.

Dr. Wanda opened her black bag. She quickly began to bandage the man's wounds.

"Mr. Lopez, can you get to the telephone?" she asked. "I need an ambulance for this man." She was pressing tightly on a bad cut to try to stop the bleeding.

(continued)

"I guess I can," Mr. Lopez said. He was pretty shaky. But he slowly crossed the room to the phone. He dialed 911. He said his name and address. Then he said, "This is an emergency." That used up all his strength.

In a few minutes, Dr. Wanda and Mr. Lopez could hear the ambulance sirens getting louder.

"Good work, Mr. Lopez. You've saved this man's life," Dr. Wanda said.

Mr. Lopez smiled. "You're the saver, not me."

When the ambulance came, the crew wasn't sure who should go to the hospital. Dr. Wanda was covered with blood. So was the man on the floor. And Mr. Lopez had fainted in his chair.

"I'm all right," Dr. Wanda said. "But these two men both need to go to the hospital." Mr. Lopez opened his eyes. But he was too weak to object.

The ambulance crew worked quickly. And in a few minutes the ambulance sped off to the hospital.

Meanwhile, Dr. Wanda picked up the phone. She called the police and reported the stabbing. She washed up in Mr. Lopez's sink. She packed her black bag.

Then she went next door to see about the baby who was still screaming.

Story 5: Exercise

Fill in the blanks with the best answer.

1. **Main Idea:** This story is about

   _____

2. **Details:** Dr. Wanda tried to cover Mr. Lopez's broken windows with

   _____

   And she made him some

   _____

3. **Sequence:** There was a fight in the hall. Then,

   _____

   fell into Mr. Lopez's room.

4. **Cause and Effect:** The woman dropped the knife because

   _____

5. **Drawing Conclusions:** The teenagers like Dr. Wanda a lot because

   _____

6. **Activity:** Write one page about a person who listens to you when you
   need to talk.
   or
   Write about some time when you had to go to the doctor.

Unit 8

Community Words

Survival Vocabulary Stories

Story 1

"This week, we are going to work on reports about our town," Mr. Sanders said. The kids looked bored.

"Don't you think reports are boring, Mr. Sanders?" Tim asked.

"Well, no. I think they can be fun." Mr. Sanders smiled. "The way we're going to do them will be fun." The kids seemed more interested. "We're going to work in pairs. Each pair will have a place to visit. First, you have to make up questions to ask."

"Like an interview?" Alan asked.

"Yes. Like you're a TV reporter," Mr. Sanders said. "You can decide how you want to tell the class what you learn. Maybe we could make a small news show. Like a news magazine."

"That's a great idea," Ann said. "When do we choose our topic?"

"Right now," said Mr. Sanders. A few minutes later, the students were paired up. Each pair had a topic and was busy making up twenty questions for an interview.

Mr. Sanders walked around and helped the kids write questions. He gave each student a field trip permit. The kids had to get their parents to sign it so that they could leave school to do their project.

During that week, the students went all over town, learning about their community.

The following week, they began to tell what they had learned.

Stanley and Salina went first.

(continued)

"We went to the big factory on First Street," Stanley said.

"It's the oldest factory in our town," Salina added. "They have been making shoes there since 1900. They hire a hundred thirty workers and have fifty more who do some stitching at home."

"It's a very clean factory," Stanley said. "And it has a good record for safety."

"Thank you, Stanley and Salina," Mr. Sanders said. "Terry and Ron?"

"We went to the garage on Maple Avenue," Ron said. "It is one of three garages in town. It's the newest and the smallest."

"They fix only American cars," Terry said. "They have a lot of computer equipment. It helps them figure out what's wrong with a car."

"Yeah. They said that knowing about computers really helps a mechanic these days," Stanley added. "People from all over the area are taking their car to Amfix," Stanley said. "That's the name of the garage. We'll tell you more after we go back. They're going to tune up my car for free!"

"That's great," Mr. Sanders said. "Eric and Joe, tell us about the laundry."

"I'm going to let Joe tell you," Eric said. "He spent a whole day there last Saturday. I just went on our interview time."

"Why did you spend the whole day?" Mr. Sanders asked. "Are you going to start your own laundry business?"

"I might," Joe said. "Or I'd like to work at Chen's Laundry. The Chen family came from China fifty years ago. The laundry has been passed down from father to son. The Chens are very proud of the business. They do all the laundry for the restaurants in town and for the hospital. Also, they have about fifty families who always bring their laundry to them."

(continued)

"That's a lot of dirty clothes," said Eric. "They have big washers and dryers. And they have the biggest ironing boards I've ever seen. They call them *mangles*. You have to be careful using the mangles. If not, you can burn yourself."

"Speaking of burns," Joe said, "it is very hot in the laundry, even in winter. It is very clean, too. The best part was that I got to eat egg rolls with the Chens at lunchtime."

"Now we know why you went there on Saturday," Mr. Sanders laughed.

"Can we give our report next?" Robin asked.

"Sure," Mr. Sanders said. "You went to the pharmacy, didn't you?"

"Yes. Kirsten and I went to the old brick pharmacy on Main Street. It's been Swan's pharmacy since 1935. Before that, it was the town dry goods store. The sidewalk in front is made out of old stones."

"What's a dry goods store?" Joe asked.

"It's a store that sold just about everything back in the old days," Kirsten said.

"All the kids bought penny candy there. Their moms bought flour and sugar and fabric. Their dads bought seeds for the garden and pipe tobacco. The barber used to cut hair in the back room," Kirsten said.

"When the first food store opened in 1935, Mr. Swan changed his store into a pharmacy. He put in a soda fountain so he could sell ice cream and coffee. Then he started selling vitamins and health products."

"Mr. Swan is not there anymore. But the soda fountain is still there. Kirsten and I tried ice cream sodas. Boy, were they good," Robin said.

"Did anyone visit the theater yet?" Mr. Sanders asked.

(continued)

"We did," said Ann and Harry at the same time.

"First, we talked to the owner, Ms. Samson. She showed us the room where they run the movies," Ann said.

"There's not much to see," Harry added.

"But I learned some new things about the building. It once was a place for ballroom dancing. And during World War II, the Red Cross used the building to store bandages."

"Ms. Samson took over the place in 1980. She made it into a theater," Ann said.

"She had to do a lot of work to change it into a theater. Now she's thinking about making it into a mall."

"She's *cool*," Harry said. "She gave us movie tickets for the whole class."

The class started to cheer. "Hold on," Mr. Sanders said. "We need to hear one last report. Who else is ready to talk?"

"We are," James said. "Alex and I went to the old school on Maple Street."

"We talked to the superintendent first," Alex said. "He told us the story of the first school. Until 1900, all the kids went to the one-room school on Pine Street."

"When the shoe factory opened," James said, "more people moved to town. So the town had to build the school on Maple Street. It has high ceilings and shiny wood floors. It's not used as a school anymore. But the school department stores supplies there."

"That's all we have found out so far," Alex said.

Story 1: Exercise

Circle the letter of the best answer.

1. **Main Idea:** This story is about

    (a) a field trip to town

    (b) a class project to study the town

    (c) a TV show about old places

2. **Details:** The kids had to make up

    (a) twenty-five questions

    (b) thirty questions

    (c) twenty questions

3. **Sequence:** First, the kids made up questions. Then

    (a) they visited a place in the town

    (b) they had their parents sign a form

    (c) they met as a group

4. **Cause and Effect:** The factory opened up. Then

    (a) more people moved to town

    (b) everyone had a job

    (c) boys and girls quit school to go to work

5. **Drawing Conclusions:** Most kids liked this project because

    (a) they got out of school

    (b) they liked working together

    (c) they liked doing reports

6. **Activity:** Ask someone about a building in your community. Make up ten questions. Write down what you learn. Share the information with your class.

Story 2

"Mr. Sanders, can we finish our reports today?" Julia asked. A lot of the kids were talking. No one wanted to work.

"Settle down, class. It's time to get started," Mr. Sanders said. "Julia is right. Today we hear the last reports. Tim and Alan, where did you go?"

"We visited the church on North Main Street," Tim said. "It was built in 1860."

"Parts of it were," Alan said. "The steeple is new. The first one blew down fifty years ago in a snowstorm."

"At the corner of the building is a stone with names carved on it. The people named on the stone were the founders of the church. I found my great-great-grandfather's name on it. My parents didn't even know about that," Tim said.

"So your family has lived here a long time," Mr. Sanders said. "That's interesting. Let's move on. Who studied the synagogue?"

"We did," Dawn said, pointing at Becky.

"What is a synagogue?" Alex asked.

"It's a place where Jewish people worship," Dawn said.

"It's one of the newest buildings in town. Jewish people used to have to travel to Dover to go to the synagogue there."

"Five years ago, a group built the synagogue here," Becky added.

(continued)

"It's also called a *temple*. It's very nice inside. The person who is in charge is called a *rabbi*. He let us look around. And he told us about the Jewish beliefs. Dawn and I are going to a service there. Then we'll tell you more about it."

"We're next," Ross said. "Lars and I went to the library. I've been in the library a hundred times. But I never knew anything about it."

"Me either," Lars said. "It turns out that one woman, Mrs. Barton, gave all the money to build the library. Her husband owned the shoe factory that Stanley and Salina visited. His picture hangs over the main desk. His wife loved to read. So after her husband died, she had the library built."

"She picked out all the books for the original library," Ross said. "They're still there in a small room on the first floor. The town took over the library when Mrs. Barton died."

"We're going back to look at Mrs. Barton's books," Lars said. "We want to find out what kind of books women read back in those days."

"That should be fun," Mr. Sanders said. "Chip and Todd, do you want to tell us about your trip to the barbershop?"

The class laughed, as two boys with very long hair stood up.

"We picked the best place to go," Chip said. "The barber, Mr. Romano, was really nice. He didn't even try to talk us into getting haircuts. He told us a lot about barbers in the old days. They used to take out people's teeth and do small operations on people."

"Do any barbers still do that?" Ann asked.

"Not in this country," Todd said. "You have to go to school before you can be a dentist or a doctor. You have to go to school to be a barber, too. Mr. Romano went to school in New York City. But he wanted to work in a smaller town. So he came here in 1970. He's been here ever since."

"Now to hear from the bankers," Mr. Sanders said, looking around the room.

(continued)

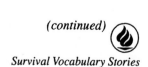

Scott and Rocko stood up. They had wads of dollar bills in their hands. They gave one to Mr. Sanders. Then they started passing them out to the kids.

The kids began to laugh. Rocko's picture was on one side of the bill. Scott's picture was on the other. The boys smiled.

"We fooled you for a minute, didn't we?" Rocko asked.

"You sure did," Mr. Sanders said.

"Don't try to spend these," Scott said. "Ms. Wills, the banker, said if we wanted to copy a real dollar bill, we had to make it bigger or smaller than a real one. These are a little bigger than a real one."

"Let's hear about the bank," Mr. Sanders said, "*not* how to make dollar bills."

"The bank has been in town for a long time. It used to be over near the post office. In 1960 they built a new building," Rocko said.

"Ms. Wills didn't tell us too much about the bank. But she did tell us about one big holdup they had," Scott said.

"Someone wearing a mask held up the bank just after a big shipment of money had come in. No one got hurt. But the robber got away with a hundred thousand dollars."

"Did they ever catch the robber?" Ross asked.

"Nope. And none of the money ever showed up," Rocko said.

"Some people think the money might be hidden somewhere in town. Maybe the robber never dared to spend it."

"We're going to dig up the old newspaper stories on the robbery. We're going to try to solve the crime," Scott said. "If you want to help us, see me after class." The kids all began to talk.

(continued)

"All right, class. Let's listen to our last report. Wes and Mark, please tell us about the post office."

"OK," said Mark. "We'll try to make this short. Right, Wes?"

Wes nodded. "Yeah. The post office hasn't been robbed. Not like the bank," Wes said.

"But, there is one funny thing about it. Did you ever wonder why we had such a big post office? The town is not very big. But the post office is huge," Mark said.

"It seems that there was a mistake back in 1978. Our post office was supposed to be built in Littleton, Colorado. The money came to Littleton, New Hampshire, instead. So our town got the big post office. The other Littleton got the small one," Wes stated.

"That's a pretty big mix-up," Stanley said.

"Once they started building, no one could do anything about it. Our town can handle up to fifty thousand pieces of mail each day," Mark said.

"And we have space for post office boxes for several thousand people. We'll tell you more facts about the post office later," Wes added.

"OK, class. Good job. I'm looking forward to hearing more from all of you. What do you think of trying to build a model of the town?"

Just then the bell rang. "Maybe we can talk about it tomorrow."

Before Mr. Sanders could finish, kids were crowding around Scott and Rocko. The plans to solve the bank robbery were under way.

Story 2: Exercise

Choose the best answer.

1. **Main Idea:** A good title for this story is

   (a) Class Reports

   (b) Our Town

   (c) A Town History

2. **Details:** The boys passed out dollar bills that had _____

   picture on one side and _____
   picture on the other.

3. **Sequence:** First, Tim and Alan talked about the church. Then Dawn and Becky talked about the

   _____

4. **Cause and Effect:** Rocko and Scott saw all the money at the bank. Then

   _____

5. **Drawing Conclusions:** The boys and girls in this class learned a lot because

   _____

6. **Activity:** Choose a place in your town and try to find out about it.

Story 3

"This is Joy Grendel. I'm standing on the sidewalk in front of Swan's pharmacy. I'm reporting live on the big Thanksgiving Day Parade. Police officers are making sure cars don't drive down the street where the parade is lining up. Let's talk to some of the people watching. Sir. Excuse me, sir."

"Yeah?" said one man, who continued to stare at the parade lineup.

"I'm Joy Grendel from WXQR TV. Are you having a good time?"

"Not yet. Nothing has happened so far."

"Right. Well, why are you here?"

"My son is playing the drum in the school band. I can't wait to hear him play."

"What about the floats. Does your company have a float in the parade?"

"No. I'm a plumber. I work with floats. But not the kind that are in a parade."

"Thank you, sir. Let's move on to this little girl. Hello. What's your name?"

"Cwissy."

"Hi, Chrissy. Do you like the parade?"

"No. Wanna go home," and she started to cry.

"You scared my little girl," said a woman, who swooped up Chrissy and glared at Joy.

"Sorry. I didn't mean to," Joy replied. "This is quite an afternoon, isn't it?"

(continued)

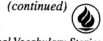

"Quite. I try to make a quick trip to the laundry. I park my car in the parking garage. Now I can't move. I am stuck until the parade is over."

"That's too bad. Cheer up. I hear some band music. The parade is coming."

"Mommy! Wanna go home," the little girl cried.

"Chrissy, look. Here comes a truck with Santa in the back." Joy pointed up the street. Chrissy put her hands over her eyes.

"Don't wanna look."

Joy walked down the street. "This is Joy Grendel, talking to you live from downtown Littleton. Here comes the first float. Looks like it was built by the shoe factory. It is made out of lots and lots of shoe boxes. It has a giant boot in the middle of it."

"S'cuse me," a man with several children said to Joy. "My kids can't see."

"Sorry. I'm Joy Grendel from WXQR TV. Would you like to say anything to our viewers?"

"I think everyone in town is *here*. No one's at home watching." But he waved at the camera and said, "Hi there."

"Look, Daddy! Here comes the float your bank made." One of the little kids tugged on his father's sleeve.

"The little brick building actually has a revolving door. That's a nice float," Joy said.

(continued)

"It better be. It cost plenty. Do you know what it took to make that silver dollar sign on the top? One hundred rolls of aluminum foil!"

$

"Wow, " Joy said.

"We won first place," the banker said. "Look at that big blue ribbon." The crowd clapped and cheered.

Joy walked up the street, past the library, and over to the barber shop.

The parade went all the way from the fire station to the mall.

"The parade goes almost all the way across the town. It's quite a sight," Joy said.

"Here's the superintendent of public works. Tell me, Mr. Parks, do you think you'll have much of a cleanup after the parade?"

Mr. Parks looked around. "Maybe a few pieces of aluminum foil and a couple of shoe box tops. But people are pretty good nowadays. Or maybe they just don't want to pay a fine for littering."

"Well, the parade will be finishing soon," Joy said. "A restaurant in the shopping mall is offering hot drinks to everyone who was in the parade."

She was interrupted by the sound of fire sirens wailing.

"Those sirens tell us the last parade unit has left the fire station. This is Joy Grendel for WXQR TV. I'm standing in front of the synagogue on Main Street. I'll say good-bye now."

Name _____

Date _____

Story 3: Exercise

Circle the letter of the best answer.

1. **Main Idea:** A good title for this story is

   (a) The Parade

   (b) The TV Reporter

   (c) The Thanksgiving Day Parade

2. **Details:** It took one hundred rolls of aluminum foil to make

   (a) the silver dollar sign

   (b) the fake panda bear

   (c) the mailbox

3. **Sequence:** Joy talked to the banker. Then she talked to

   (a) the plumber

   (b) Chrissy

   (c) the superintendent of public works

4. **Cause and Effect:** Chrissy's mother will stay in town until the parade ends because

   (a) there is a snowstorm

   (b) Chrissy loves parades

   (c) her car is blocked by the parade

5. **Drawing Conclusions:** You can tell that parade day is a big day for the town because

   (a) Joy Grendel says so

   (b) everyone in town is there to watch

   (c) there is only one parade each year

Story 4

Ben Otis was on a trip with his mom and dad. The family had been driving for days and days. Ben was tired and bored. He missed his friends. His birthday was in two days. No party for him this year. He was mad about that.

They had just eaten dinner in a restaurant. Mrs. Otis stopped to pick out some postcards. "Look at this," she said to Ben.

"What?" asked Ben. Another dull place to visit, I bet, he said to himself.

"It's a ghost town not very far from here," his mom said. "Let's ask Dad if he wants to go see it."

"Wow. This looks pretty cool," Ben said. "Can we go there, Dad?"

"Let's see," Mr. Otis said. "How about if we go there for your birthday? Tomorrow we want to see some Indian caves. The next day we could go to the ghost town."

"Great," Ben said. "Finally something *I* want to do!"

The next day they stopped at the post office. They put their postcards in the mailbox.

"Grandma will be glad to get some mail," Mrs. Otis said. They had gone a few steps down the sidewalk when Mrs. Otis said, "I forgot to go to the pharmacy for some sunscreen. Can we go back and get some?"

"Are you sure you don't want to stop at the mall, too?" Mr. Otis kidded his wife.

"Or maybe get some books from the library?" Ben asked. "What do you need sunscreen for anyway? We're going to be in *caves*!"

"You two just hush," Mrs. Otis said. Back they went to the pharmacy.

(continued)

"Now are we ready, Mom?" Ben asked. Off they went for a day of going deep into some Indian caves. Ben went to sleep that night and dreamed of Indians riding across the plains.

"Happy birthday, Ben," his dad said in the morning.

"Thanks, Dad. How soon are we leaving for the ghost town?" Ben asked.

"Well, I thought I'd take the car to the garage. Your mother wants to go to church. And it looks like you need a trip to the barber's."

"Dad, you're too much. Let's get going. Mom, are you ready?"

"As soon as we find a bank where I can cash a check," his mom said.

"Oh brother," Ben said. "If I'm lucky, I'll get to see this ghost town before my *next* birthday."

"Cheer up, Son," Mr. Otis said, patting Ben on the back. "I know right where the bank is. The hard part is finding the ghost town."

"Why did I have to get you guys for parents?" Ben groaned.

After a stop at the bank, Mr. Otis asked a police officer how to get to the ghost town.

"Go left by the button factory. Pass the synagogue on your right. Then make a right turn by the fire station. It's just about fifteen miles. You can't miss it."

"Thanks a lot," Mr. Otis said.

"No problem," said the police officer.

Ben sat up front. He made sure his dad took the correct turns. They drove for about half an hour. Up ahead they could see some old buildings. When they got closer, there was a sign telling them where to park. From the parking lot, an old man drove them in a wagon into the ghost town. An old mule pulled the wagon.

(continued)

"I'm Gabby Hayes," the old man said. "Pleased to meet you."

"This is neat," Ben said. His mom and dad smiled.

The wagon stopped in front of the Deadwood Theater. An old sign on the front told them that at 10:00 they could see a video about the town.

"Let's do that," Ben said, looking at his watch. "We just have time to make it."

"OK," said his mom and dad. They went into the theater. The seats were covered with faded red velvet. A small fan whirred. The air smelled of popcorn.

In a few minutes the lights went down. A movie played on the screen. It showed each building in town and gave a short story about it.

"Doesn't that voice sound like our wagon driver's?" Ben asked.

"It sure does," his mom said.

"Shhhh. You'll miss the story," his dad said.

Soon, the video ended. "I like this place," Ben said. "The kids here didn't have to go to school."

"Yes, but look how many of them turned into outlaws and bad guys," Mr. Otis said. They walked out into the sunlight. They all blinked. The wagon driver came out of the theater behind them.

"Did you like the show?" he asked.

"Yes, we did. Was that you talking?" Ben asked.

"Yup," the old man said. He smiled. "I'm kind of the superintendent around here. I do everything from sweeping the floors to driving the wagon. At lunchtime you'll find me slinging hash in the restaurant. Well, so long. Enjoy your stay." He got into the wagon and drove back to the parking lot.

(continued)

"It looks like we have the place to ourselves," Mrs. Otis said.

"Let's get going," said Ben. "I want to see where Billy the Kid spent the night."

"Me, too," said his dad. "I also want to check out the graveyard."

"I'll meet you there in a few minutes. I want to stop in the ladies' room," said Mrs. Otis. "I hope old Gabby Hayes is a good plumber." They all laughed.

Ben and his dad walked to the end of the street. A small graveyard with a few broken headstones was off to one side. An old fence surrounded it.

"Not much to see," Ben said.

"Let's look at the stones," his dad said. "Maybe there are some famous outlaws buried here." He pushed open the old gate. They walked in. At the third headstone, Mr. Otis stopped.

"What is it, Dad?" Ben asked.

"Look at this. It says Benjamin Otis on this stone. And whoever he was was born on this very day—your birthday," his dad said. "We must have had a relative who was an outlaw."

"You're joking," Ben said. "That's too weird." He stared at his name and month and day of birth on the old gravestone. "I'm spooked," he said. "Let's get out of this graveyard."

Just then, Mrs. Otis came up behind them. "*Boo!*" she said before they saw her. They all jumped. And then they all laughed.

"Don't tell me the ladies' room had a ghost, too." Mr. Otis said.

"As a matter of fact . . ." Mrs. Otis said, as they headed back toward the town to see a few more ghosts.

Story 4: Exercise

Circle the letter of the best answer.

1. **Main Idea:** A good title for this story is

    (a) Ghost Town Birthday

    (b) A Long Trip

    (c) Ghosts

2. **Details:** Mrs. Otis went to the pharmacy for

    (a) stamps

    (b) sunglasses

    (c) sunscreen

3. **Sequence:** After the movie, Mrs. Otis went

    (a) to the pharmacy

    (b) to the ladies' room

    (c) to the graveyard

4. **Cause and Effect:** Ben was tired and bored because

    (a) they had been driving for days

    (b) he had been sick

    (c) he missed his friends

5. **Drawing Conclusions:** Ben felt spooked because

    (a) he was afraid of ghosts

    (b) his name and month and day of birth were on a gravestone

    (c) the town was not on a main road

Survival Vocabulary Stories

Story 5

"Now that you have learned about our town," Ms. Pash said, "let's try to plan a new town.

Ms. Pash was the shop teacher. She had the same kids Mr. Sanders had. The kids recently had finished their reports on the town for Mr. Sanders.

"Our town grew before we had a plan. That's why we have an old factory near new houses. What other buildings are in the wrong place?" Ms. Pash asked.

"I think the garage is too near the houses, too," Tim said.

"Why is that bad?" Ms. Pash asked.

"The noise and the smell of the oil are bad," Tim said. "I know. I live near there."

"I would put the fire station somewhere else," Alex said.

"It is next door to the church. On Sunday, when there's a fire, you can't hear anything in church."

"That's true," Ms. Pash said. "Now, I want you to work in groups. We'll cut the town into four parts. First, we'll make a map of the town the way it is today. Next, we'll vote on what to change. Last, we'll make new maps and a small model of the town."

She divided the class into four groups. Each group took one part of town.

Alex and Terry's group had the part with the pharmacy, the laundry, a school, and a lot of houses.

(continued)

155

Tim and Stanley's group had the downtown part. They had the post office, restaurants, bank, and library.

Wes and Todd's group had the barbershop, a school, the superintendent's office, and the theater.

Ron and Kirsten's group had the synagogue, the plumber's shop, the high school, and a lot of houses.

Each day, the kids worked on their maps. Shop class seemed to go by faster than usual.

Stanley cut out small paper houses to put right on the map. His group drew the sidewalk and roads with a black marker.

In front of the post office, they made a small mailbox. It had a bag of mail next to it. They even put some books in front of the library.

On the corner by the theater, Todd drew a small police officer who held up her hand to stop cars.

He put a red-and-white-striped pole outside the barbershop. Wes drew the playground outside the school.

The other two groups used green paper to show grass and blue paper to show swimming pools.

Ms. Pash was pleased with the way the class worked on this project.

Each group told the rest of the class about their section of town. They talked about what was good and bad in their part.

Soon, it was time to plan the new town.

(continued)

"I think we can put all the shops in one mall. Then we can put the houses all around the mall," Tim said.

"Where would you put schools?" Ann asked.

"Maybe one school at each corner of the town," Tim said. "Those four schools would be for the little kids. I'd put one big high school in the middle of town."

"I don't like that idea," Ann said. "Think of going to school in the middle of downtown. Where would we put our playing fields?"

"It would be hard to find a place to park," Kirsten said.

"What if we put houses in the middle, then put all the shops and factories all around the houses?" Todd asked. "Schools could be in the part where the houses are."

"Class, what do you think of that idea?" Ms. Pash asked.

"I don't think that will work," Lars said. "The post office, the fire station, and the police station should be near the middle of town. Then they're close to all the people who need them. Put the factories outside of town."

"I think we're forgetting something," Julia said. "What about the lake and all the forests outside of town? We want to be careful to take care of that land space."

"That's a good point," Ms. Pash said. "For homework, each of you can draw out your best plan for the town. We'll talk some more tomorrow."

Story 5: Exercise

Fill in the blanks with the best answer.

1. **Main Idea:** This story is about a class that is

   _____

2. **Details:** The garage is too close to

   _____

3. **Sequence:** First, the class makes a map of the town the way it is now. Next, the class will

   _____

4. **Cause and Effect:** If the high school is in the middle of town, then

   _____

5. **Drawing Conclusions:** Planning a town is (a) easy, (b) hard because

   _____

6. **Activity:** Draw a map of your town or your neighborhood. Show as many buildings from the following list below as you can.

factory	synagogue	restaurant
garage	church	theater
laundry	barbershop	bank
pharmacy	fire station	school
post office	library	mall

Unit 9

Restaurant Words

Story 1

Karla and Lily went shopping at the mall. They were looking for school clothes. By lunchtime they had spent a lot of money—not just on clothes but on video games, too. Lily had five bags to carry. Karla had six.

"Let's eat lunch somewhere else," Karla said. "Do you know any good restaurants?"

"No," Lily said. "We can just try one. As long as it has a booth big enough for us and our bags!" They left the mall to look for a restaurant.

"That place looks good," Karla pointed to a small building next to the theater. "Let's see if we need a reservation."

"I don't think we will," said Lily. "They seem to have some empty tables and some seats at the counter."

"Check out the menu taped on the door," Karla said. "I hope they have pasta."

"Hurry," Lily said. "I have to use the ladies' room." They opened the door and walked in. A sign said "Please be seated."

"You go sit down. I'll join you in a minute." Lily followed signs that said "Restrooms." Karla sat at a booth by the window. She liked to be able to watch people walking by on the sidewalk. A waitress with a white apron on came to the table.

"Are you ready to order?" she asked. She put a placemat and napkin on the table.

"I'd like to wait for my friend," Karla said.

"OK," the waitress said. "You can go to the salad bar while you're waiting."

(continued)

"Thanks," Karla smiled. "That will be my appetizer." She slid out of the booth without looking. *Bang.* She ran right into a waiter carrying a tray full of dishes. The waiter dropped the tray. Dishes crashed everywhere.

"Oh dear. I'm so sorry," Karla said. She started picking up the dishes.

The waiter said, "My fault. I didn't look where I was going."

Just then Lily came back. "Looks like you've been busy," she said to Karla.

"Why don't you girls go sit in another booth," the waitress said. "Then we can get this cleaned up." Karla and Lily picked up all their bags and moved to a booth across the room.

"So how was the ladies' room?" Karla asked Lily.

Lily started to laugh. "I don't know," she said. "I ended up in the *men's* room by mistake. Lucky for me, there wasn't anyone else in there."

Karla started to laugh, too. The waitress came to take their order. They tried to stop giggling.

"I'd like pasta with clam sauce and some espresso for dessert," Karla said.

"Same for me," Lily said. "I'm still in a state of shock after my trip to the men's room." The girls started to giggle again. When the food came, they ate every bite.

"I had no idea I was so hungry," Karla said. "Let's see if we can order a takeout sandwich. We may be hungry again before we get home." When the waitress brought their check, they asked her for a pocket sandwich. She added that order to the check. Shortly afterward she brought them a bag with their sandwich in it.

"I bet they're glad to get rid of *us*!" Lily said, as they left the restaurant.

"Next time, we must try to behave better," Karla said, laughing.

Story 1: Exercise

Fill in the blanks with the best answer.

1. **Main Idea:** This story is about

_____

_____

2. **Details:** Karla sat

_____

3. **Sequence:** As Karla got up to go to the salad bar, she

_____

4. **Cause and Effect:** The waiter ran right into Karla and

_____

5. **Drawing Conclusions:** You can tell the girls had a good time because

_____

Story 2

Pam had a new job. She was working as a waitress. She went to work at 10:00 in the morning. The restaurant opened at 11:00. Every day she did the same things when she first got to work.

She made sure her booths were clean. She filled the napkin holder. Then she put menus at each booth or table. She wiped off the countertops. Finally, she checked the salad bar. She made sure the lettuce was fresh. She put a pile of clean bowls at one end.

While Pam did these jobs, another waitress cleaned the ladies' room and lounge. One of the waiters cleaned the men's room. He also swept the sidewalk outside the front entrance. They all answered the phone to take reservations.

Pam's first week was long. She tried hard to do things right. Each day something bad happened. On Monday, she got her orders mixed up. She gave sandwiches to the people who ordered salad. She gave soup to the people who wanted sandwiches.

"Don't worry," her boss said. "You'll do better tomorrow."

On Tuesday, she gave people their appetizers. But she forgot to take them their meal. She forgot to ask people if they wanted dessert. She spilled water all over one table.

"Don't worry," her boss said. "You'll do better tomorrow." Pam looked sad.

On Wednesday, she dropped a tray full of dishes. Lots of plates broke. When she tried to sweep up the mess, she slipped and fell.

(continued)

     Survival Vocabulary Stories

"Don't worry," her boss said. "Everyone makes mistakes at first." Pam picked herself up.

On Thursday, she kept adding up her checks wrong. People were mad because she charged them too much. Once, she gave the check to the wrong table. Someone called to order some takeout chicken. She put takeout pork in the bag by mistake. Pam was ready to quit.

"Don't worry," her boss said. "You'll do better tomorrow. And it's payday."

I'll never do better, Pam said to herself. I don't think I'm cut out to be a waitress. Maybe I'll quit.

Friday she came in to work early. She did all her chores. Then she helped one of the other waitresses. She worked all through lunch with no mistakes. One man told her what a good waitress she was. He left her a big tip.

This isn't so bad, she said to herself. The afternoon was slow. So she helped put salt and pepper in all the shakers. She cut peppers and onions for the salad bar. She helped make the batter for cakes. The day flew by. Before she knew it, it was time for dinner. She got all her orders right the first time. She carried her tray with one hand. She added up all her checks right.

When it was quitting time, Pam had a big smile on her face. Her pocket was full of tips. She hadn't made any mistakes. Her boss was smiling, too. She handed Pam a green paycheck.

"I knew you could do it," she said. "You're one of my best workers."

"Thank you for giving me a chance," Pam said. "I was ready to quit. But you were right. I did get better." She put her paycheck in her handbag. "See you on Monday," she said.

Name _____

Date _____

Story 2: Exercise

Circle the letter of the best answer.

1. **Main Idea:** A good title for this story is

   (a) Pam Makes a Mistake

   (b) Pam Learns to Be a Waitress

   (c) Pam Quits Her Job

2. **Details:** On Wednesday,

   (a) Pam got her orders mixed up

   (b) Pam forgot to go to work

   (c) Pam dropped a tray full of dishes

3. **Sequence:** When Pam got to work, she cleaned her booths and then

   (a) filled the napkin holder

   (b) cleaned the men's room

   (c) answered the telephone

4. **Cause and Effect:** Pam got a big tip because

   (a) she was lucky

   (b) the man was rich

   (c) she did a good job

5. **Drawing Conclusions:** Pam's boss didn't fire her because

   (a) she knew Pam was just learning

   (b) she liked Pam

   (c) she was a nice person

6. **Activity:** Tell about a job you had where you made some mistakes.

Story 3

Prom night was beginning. All over town, girls and boys were getting dressed up in their best clothes. Shiny cars were waiting outside to take them to the best restaurants.

Dean picked up Betty at 7:00. They had reservations for dinner at 7:30. They drove out to the Homestead Inn.

A man in a white jacket opened the door for Betty. He let Dean get out.

Then he parked the car.

Dean and Betty were a little early. They waited in the lounge. They decided to order some sparkling water. The waiter brought the glasses out on a small tray. He put a napkin next to each glass.

"It will be a few minutes until your table is ready," the waiter said. "That's good," said Betty, "because our friends haven't come yet."

Just then Val and her date, Leroy, entered the lounge. "Happy prom night to all," said Leroy.

Val and Betty said they liked each other's dresses. Then they looked at the boys. "Nice to see you guys dressed up for once," Betty said.

Both boys started to say something back. But Betty spoke first. "Come on, Val. Let's go check out the ladies' room."

"No wonder there's always a line at the ladies' room," Dean said. "The girls always have to go together."

Leroy laughed. "You're right. Then they stay in there for half an hour. I bet they don't get back before our table is ready."

But the girls came back just as the waitress said their table was ready.

(continued)

Their table was by a window. It had a white tablecloth and dark blue napkins. Outside, the sun was setting over the lake.

"Look at that gorgeous sunset," Val said.

"This table has the greatest view," Betty said.

"Nothing but the best," Dean said. "Now aren't you glad you didn't stay in the ladies' room all night?"

A waiter came to the table before Betty could answer.

"Hello. My name is Ramon." He put menus in front of each person. "Would you like an appetizer before dinner?"

Dean and Betty ordered soup. Leroy and Val ordered stuffed mushrooms.

The waiter came back with their appetizers. He took their orders for dinner. He filled their glasses with water.

"This is almost as good as the school cafeteria," Leroy joked.

"I think the food is just a *bit* better," Val said.

"Oh, I don't know," Dean said. "I was hoping to have a soggy cheese sandwich. I'll have to eat pasta supreme instead."

They finished their appetizers. The waiter brought salads. Outside it was getting dark. Lights flashed on boats out on the lake.

"I hope we make it to the prom," Betty said. "It looks like dinner is going to take a while."

"If you don't make any more stops in the ladies' room, we should make it," Dean said.

(continued)

"We're going to time you in the men's room," Val said. A band in the lounge started to play.

"We can always stay *here* and dance," Betty said.

"No way. I'm not missing the prom," Dean said. "After all those car washes to raise money—no way," he said again.

The waiter brought the main course. The kids took their time eating. They didn't leave anything on their plates.

"That was wonderful. But I'm stuffed," said Betty. "I think I'll have a cup of espresso. But no dessert."

"I'll call the waiter," Leroy said. The other kids nodded.

When the cups were empty, Dean asked the waiter for the check.

Val looked at Betty. Betty looked at Dean.

"You girls go ahead to the ladies' room," Dean said. We'll pay the bill, go to the men's room, and still beat you to the car."

Leroy gave Dean a high five. The girls ignored them. They left the table.

"Let's trick the boys," Betty said. "Let's skip the ladies' room. Dean gave me the keys to keep in my purse. We'll get the man at the door to get the car."

"Yeah!" Val said. "We'll show them who has got all the good moves!"

Story 3: Exercise

Answer in complete sentences.

1. **Main Idea:** Make up a good title for this story:

   _____

2. **Details:** What restaurant did Dean and Betty and Leroy and Val go to?

   _____

3. **Sequence:** The kids finished eating. Then

   _____

4. **Cause and Effect:** Why does Dean think there is always a long line in the ladies' room?

   _____

5. **Drawing Conclusions:** Why do the girls decide to skip the ladies' room?

   _____

Survival Vocabulary Stories

Story 4

Rod and Leon were mad. Their parents wouldn't let them go on the class trip. They said it cost too much money.

Rod and Leon decided to pretend to go to school. Instead, they skipped school. They rode a bus to the beach.

They played catch and made sand castles all morning. By noontime, they were ready to eat. They were also sunburned.

"Let's go to the mall. First, we can have lunch. Then we can play video games all afternoon," Rod said. "We'll take a bus home about the time school gets out."

"What if someone sees us?" Leon asked.

"Who will see us? All the teachers are at school. The rest of our class is spending the day in Seattle," Rod said. "Don't worry."

"OK," Leon said. "I sure am hungry."

They put on their sunglasses. They rode the bus to the mall.

They decided to go to a family restaurant. There they wouldn't need a reservation.

At the entrance they stopped.

"What if we meet a family friend?" Leon asked.

"Look the other way fast," Rod said. "Come on. Don't be such a nerd."

They kept their sunglasses on. They walked quickly into the restaurant. Rod wanted to sit in a booth. Leon wanted to sit at the counter.

"No one can see us in a booth," Rod said.

(continued)

"Yeah, but the waitress can take our order faster at the counter," Leon said. "Maybe we should order takeout."

"No, let's take a booth," Rod said.

Leon finally stopped arguing. He decided to go to the men's room before they ordered. He walked to the back of the restaurant, looking this way and that. He didn't see anyone he knew.

But with his dark glasses on, he couldn't see where he was going. *Boom!* Leon bumped right into a man coming out of the men's room. It was Rod's father!

Leon looked down and mumbled, "Excuse me." Then he rushed into the men's room. He stayed there for a few minutes. Maybe Rod's father would leave the restaurant.

"Where have you been?" Rod asked when Leon returned to the booth. "Did you see my father?"

"I sure did. I bumped into him," Leon said. "But he didn't know it was me."

"I put the menu up in front of my face," Rod said. "That was a close call."

"Let's eat and get out of here," Leon said.

"Yeah. Let's skip the soup and appetizers," Leon said. He handed Leon the menu.

"I want something big and fast," Leon said. They both ordered burgers and salads.

The waitress put their food on the table. Then she looked at the boys.

"Say, aren't you supposed to be in school?" she asked.

"Uh, no. We're at the mall on a class trip," Rod said.

(continued)

171

Survival Vocabulary Stories

"Right," the waitress said.

"I don't like the way she looked at us," Leon said.

"Guess we better skip dessert. We can get some takeout ice cream," Rod said.

The waitress came with their check. They asked for ice cream to go.

"You can pick up your ice cream at the counter where you pay your bill," the waitress said. The boys got up and started for the counter.

"Uh-oh!" Rod said in a low voice. "Look who's sitting at a table by the door." The school principal and the superintendent were having lunch.

"On second thought, let's have a long dessert," Leon said. He sat back down in the booth.

"Did you change your mind about dessert?" the waitress asked them.

"Yes, we want two super big, hot-fudge banana splits," Rod said. "With carrot cake," Leon added.

"Relax, guys. I have a note for you." The waitress handed Rod a folded piece of paper. The note said, "Hi Rod. I've paid for your lunches. Don't let the principal see you. Love, Dad. P.S. Watch your step, Leon!"

"Whew," Rod said. "My dad is one cool guy."

"You can say that again," Leon said. "Those banana splits and cake we ordered should keep us here for a while!"

"We'll eat until the coast is clear," Rod laughed.

The waitress placed two huge dishes of ice cream and two tall pieces of cake on the table.

"Think you can handle all this?" she asked. She didn't wait for an answer.

Story 4: Exercise

Fill in the blank with the best answer.

1. **Main Idea:** This story is about two boys who

   _____

2. **Details:** They couldn't go on the class trip because

   _____

3. **Sequence:** First, they went to the beach. Then

   _____

4. **Cause and Effect:** They decided to stay and have dessert because

   _____

5. **Drawing Conclusions:** Rod's dad paid for their lunches because

   _____

173

Story 5

The food for the Father-Son Dinner smelled so good. The foods class was cooking the dinner. They had planned the menu. Mr. Fry, the teacher, had ordered the food. The class still had to make the home economics area look like a restaurant.

Wayne stayed late and worked hard. He helped move tables. He cleaned the counter where the food would be served. He put flowers near the entrance and on each table.

He worked with his friend Candy to fold napkins. They put reservation cards, printed in computer class, on each table. They stacked the trays to be used for carrying food out to the tables.

The kids turned another room into a lounge. They used chairs from the teachers' room. Someone brought a rug from home. They made a booth where people could check their coats.

They finished up about 5:00. Dinner was scheduled for 6:00.

Mr. Fry thanked all the kids for their help. He looked at Wayne and said, "Wayne, you have really worked hard. Your dad is coming tonight, isn't he?"

Wayne sighed. "No. My dad is away on a trip. He said he'd try to get back. But I don't think he will be here in time."

"That's too bad," Mr. Fry said. "Are you coming anyway?"

"Yes. I said I would be a waiter," Wayne said.

Mr. Fry smiled. "Good. See you later, then."

When the dinner began, Wayne was so busy he didn't have a chance to watch the entrance for his dad.

(continued)

First, he served appetizers. As soon as those plates were cleared, he served salads. Then he took orders for the main course and began serving fish or chicken.

When everyone had a main dish, he went to the kitchen. In the kitchen, he ate some sandwiches with the other waitresses and waiters.

They just had time to make a quick trip to wash up in the rest rooms. Then it was time to serve dessert. Wayne filled his tray and walked into the home economics room.

During dessert there were speeches. The principal spoke. Some kids in the foods class talked about the Father-Son Dinner. Wayne stood at the back with the other waitresses and waiters.

Mr. Fry stood up. He started to name some people who had helped with the dinner. Wayne didn't pay much attention. He was thinking about all the homework he would have to do when he got home.

All of a sudden, he heard his name. He looked up. Mr. Fry was pointing at him. Wayne turned bright red.

"This year," Mr. Fry said, "the award for best worker goes to Wayne Perez. He put in more hours than anyone else. His father couldn't be here tonight . . ."

"Yes, he could," said a voice from the entrance. Wayne looked over. There was his dad!

Wayne accepted his award. He shook Mr. Fry's hand. Then he ran back to greet his father.

"We're serving espresso in the lounge," Mr. Fry said. "Mr. Perez, why don't you take your food in there to eat? I'm sure Wayne will be glad to fix you a plate."

Wayne set up a full tray of food. He took it into the lounge. He sat down next to his father. "So, how was your trip, Dad?" Wayne asked. He began to relax and enjoy the Father-Son Dinner.

Survival Vocabulary Stories

Story 5: Exercise

Choose the best answer.

1. **Main Idea:** The best title for this story

    (a) The Father-Son Dinner

    (b) Wayne Works Hard

    (c) The Surprise

2. Write one sentence saying why you chose your answer to number 1.

    _____

3. **Details:** Wayne's dad wasn't expected to come because

    (a) he didn't like school dinners

    (b) he worked nights

    (c) he was away on a trip

4. **Sequence:** First, the kids made the room look like a restaurant. Then

    (a) they fixed a room to look like a lounge

    (b) they cooked food

    (c) they typed menus

5. **Cause and Effect:** Wayne wasn't paying attention because

    (a) he was thinking about his homework

    (b) he was tired

    (c) he wanted to go to the movies

6. **Drawing Conclusions:** Wayne began to enjoy the dinner when

    (a) he had a rest

    (b) he won the award

    (c) he sat down with his dad

Unit 10

Travel Words

Story 1

Jay was going away to school. He was going to a school in New York. Since that was all the way across the country, he planned to go by airplane. His older sister lived in New York. She said she would meet Jay at the airport. Jay was excited about the trip.

First, he needed to buy a ticket. He rode his bicycle to the travel agency. "What is the fare to New York?" he asked.

"Four hundred dollars round-trip," the agent replied.

"I only need a one-way ticket," Jay said.

"Oh," the agent said. "That will cost two hundred and twenty-five dollars."

Jay wrote a check to pay for the ticket. He looked at the map on the travel agent's wall. "Sure is a long way to New York," he said. "Must take a lot of fuel."

The agent laughed. "It does. You could take a train, you know."

"No," Jay said. "I need to get there fast."

"Well, you will," the agent said. "It will take five hours going by jet."

"That's fast. Well, thanks for the ticket. I've got to go now." Jay rode his bicycle back home. His mother helped him pack. They filled one suitcase and a big trunk. Both were very heavy. His dad was going to have the trunk shipped by truck across the country.

"What have you got in here, rocks?" his dad asked as he helped Jay lift the trunk into the car.

"I have all my things for the whole year. No wonder it's heavy," Jay said.

Soon it was the day Jay was leaving. His dad put the suitcase in the car. "Hope we don't have a flat tire," he joked.

(continued)

"Hope the plane gets off the ground," Jay's little brother added.

Jay pretended he didn't hear them. "Dad, how long will it take to get to the airport?"

"A little over an hour. That's if we don't get stuck behind a slow truck," he said. "We have plenty of time, I think."

The trip to the airport was easy. They parked in back of the airport bus. It took people from one airline to another. The driver told Jay's dad where to go for the plane Jay was taking.

A man on a motorcycle zoomed past them. "He's going too fast," Jay's dad said.

"He's a policeman," Jay's mom said. "He must be after someone."

"Let's go," Jay said. "I don't want to be late." He took the suitcase. They checked in at the ticket counter. The agent gave Jay a seat by the window. The whole family took the elevator to the upper floor. They went to the boarding area.

Jay hugged his mom and dad good-bye. He gave his little brother a high five. Then he walked down the long hallway and onto the plane. The flight attendant looked at his ticket. She told Jay where his seat was. Jay looked out the window. He waved to his parents. Then he sat back and buckled up his seat belt. Soon the plane was zooming down the runway.

Jay read an airline magazine. The flight attendant brought lunch. Then there was a video to watch. Jay left his seat once to visit the men's room. Before he knew it, they were circling New York. But then the pilot came on the loudspeaker. "Our landing will be delayed," he said. "Traffic into the airport is heavy."

"Uh, oh," Jay said. "My sister won't be very happy about a delay." They circled the airport for almost two hours. Finally the plane landed. Jay was able to get off. His sister wasn't there to meet him. Maybe she was waiting

(continued)

down where the suitcases were. He followed signs to where he could get his bag. There was his suitcase. But still no sign of his sister.

"Jay Savits, report to the TWA ticket booth," a voice said over the loudspeaker. Jay jumped when he heard his name. That must be where my sister is, he thought.

He found the ticket booth. "I'm Jay Savits," he said to the man in the booth.

"I have a note for you," the man said. Jay read the note.

"Hi, sorry I'm not there to meet you," it said. "Take a cab to the Red Bird restaurant. I'll meet you for dinner. Love, Sis."

"Oh great," Jay said.

"Is there a problem?" the ticket man asked.

"Where can I get a cab?" Jay asked.

"Right out front. But it will cost you a lot. You could take a bus to the subway."

"No, I think I'll try the cab. My sister will have to pay for it." Jay hauled his suitcase outside. He finally shared a cab with three other people. They went all over New York City. At last, they reached the Red Bird restaurant.

"Do you want me to wait?" the cab driver asked.

"Maybe you'd better. I'll make sure my sister is here," Jay said. He went to the door of the restaurant. The hostess came over to him.

"May I help you?" she asked.

"Yes, I'm meeting my sister for dinner," Jay said.

"Oh, are you Jay Savits?"

(continued)

180

"Yes," Jay said.

"I have a note for you."

"Oh no. Not another note," Jay groaned. He read the note.

"Hi," it said, "sorry I missed you. Take the subway to Lincoln Center. I have concert tickets for us. Love, Sis." Jay wanted to stay at the restaurant. He could smell the food. He was very hungry. But he went back to the cab.

"I'm supposed to take the subway to Lincoln Center. Is it far?" he asked.

"It's on the other side of town," the cab driver answered. He got Jay's suitcase out of the cab. Then he showed Jay where to buy a subway token. "The conductor on the subway will tell you where to get off. Good luck."

Jay paid him and walked down into the subway. He put his token in the slot and walked onto the train. A woman passenger told him when to get off.

Jay was very hungry by now. He walked slowly to Lincoln Center. The ticket booth was closed. He banged on the door. Soon a man came out. He looked surprised to see a boy with a suitcase.

"What can I do for you?" he asked.

"I'm supposed to meet my sister. She has my ticket."

"I don't know anything about that," the man said. "Let me go check." Just then, Jay's sister came out of the auditorium.

"Boy, am I glad to see you," she said, giving Jay a hug. "I was afraid you didn't get my notes. How was your trip?"

Jay grinned with relief. "Let's put it this way," he said. "You're not half as glad to see me as I am to see you. I feel like I've traveled on everything except a boat today. I'm ready to stop."

"Well, you have missed the concert," Sis said. "Now we have a long walk ahead of us to get to my apartment."

"That's just what I need," Jay said. "More traveling."

Story 1: Exercise

Circle the letter of the best answer.

1. **Main Idea:** This story is about a boy

   (a) who got lost

   (b) who took a trip by himself

   (c) who missed his plane

2. **Details:** Jay went to the airport

   (a) in a car

   (b) on the train

   (c) by bus

3. **Sequence:** After the plane landed, Jay

   (a) went to the men's room

   (b) called home

   (c) went to get his suitcase

4. **Cause and Effect:** Jay wanted to stay at the restaurant because

   (a) he was afraid he'd never find his sister

   (b) he was hungry

   (c) he was lost

5. **Drawing Conclusions:** The next time Jay flies to New York,

   (a) he will not plan to meet his sister

   (b) he will know what to expect

   (c) he will take more money with him

6. **Activity:** Write a sentence telling why you chose your answer to question 5.

Story 2

Carmen thought she was a pretty good driver. She was almost sixteen. She had started driver education at school. So far, she had driven all around town. Her mom usually let her drive to school in the morning.

Monday afternoon, Carmen got into the driver education car. She put on her seat belt, ready to go. Ms. Moss, the teacher, said she could start the car. Ms. Moss sat in the front seat with her seat belt on. She had a brake pedal on her side of the car, too.

Carmen drove as far as the end of the school drive. The buses were loading kids.

"Rats," said Carmen. "I can't pass the bus. Its red lights are flashing."

"Watch out for the bicycles, too," Ms. Moss said. "The kids don't always look before they ride out." Just then, a motorcycle raced past the car and the bus.

"Who is that?" Ms. Moss asked. "He's not wearing a helmet."

"Plus, he passed the bus," Carmen said. "I don't know who it was."

"He's not a very good driver," Ms. Moss said. "Must not be one of *my* students." She took a map out of the glove compartment. "Let's see where we'll drive today. Hmmm. How about down the turnpike?"

"That's OK with me," Carmen said. "I think the buses are pulling out now."

"OK, let's roll," Ms. Moss said. She sat back in her seat. "Turn left at the corner. Not too fast, now."

Carmen looked both ways. At the corner, she waited for a truck before she turned. She made two more turns. She stopped at the tollbooth to put a token in the basket. A black-and-white cab passed her on the left.

(continued)

"Whew," Carmen said. "I thought that cab was a police car."

"You don't need to worry unless you're going too fast," Ms. Moss said. They drove about five miles on the turnpike. "Take the next exit," Ms. Moss said. "We'll drive out toward the airport."

Carmen took the exit. Up ahead, there was a railroad crossing. The red lights were blinking. The crossing gate dropped.

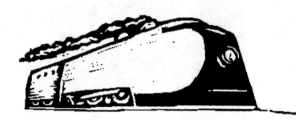

"Great," Carmen said. "This is my day to wait for flashing lights."

A long, slow train passed in front of them. "My hour will be up and I've hardly done any driving. Just a lot of waiting."

The train finally passed. The conductor stood at the back and waved to Carmen. "I think they should turn all these trains into subways," Carmen said. "Then we'd never have to wait for them."

Ms. Moss laughed. "Don't be in such a hurry," she said. "Drive out to the airport. You can try parking in the parking garage." A big airplane flew over the highway just ahead of them. It was so low Carmen thought she saw the pilot in the cockpit.

"Now what?" Carmen asked. "With my luck, one of these big planes will land on the highway in front of me."

"Watch the traffic, now. This is a busy airport," Ms. Moss said. "Turn right into the parking garage. Take a ticket from the agent." The agent waved to Ms. Moss. He was used to seeing the driver education car in the parking garage.

Carmen did what Ms. Moss said. Slowly she drove to the upper level of the garage. "I hope there's an elevator in here," she said. "I wouldn't want to have to walk this high."

"Follow the yellow arrows," Ms. Moss said. "They point to the exit. Take a right turn at the bottom of the ramp. We'll go back to school a new way."

(continued)

"I hope you have the map," Carmen said. "I don't know my way back."

"I'll tell you," Ms. Moss said. "First, cross the bridge. Then take the road that runs along the river."

"Oh. I think I've gone that way with my dad," Carmen said.

"On this road, you need to be sure to stay on your own side. There's not much room." Ms. Moss turned on the radio. Carmen watched the road carefully. After a few miles, she could see the bridge towers ahead. When they got close, Ms. Moss started to laugh.

"What's funny?" Carmen asked.

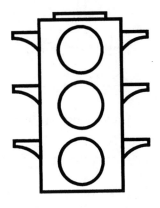

"See those flashing lights?" Ms. Moss said. "That means the drawbridge is up. A big boat must be going under."

"I give up," Carmen said. "More waiting." The boat finally passed under the bridge. Carmen was at the head of a long line of cars. She tried to go a little less than the speed limit. A red car in back of her pulled out to pass her. It was a bad place to pass. There was a double yellow line.

"That guy is going to be hurt if he drives like that," Ms. Moss said.

"That guy is in trouble right now," Carmen said. She slowed down and pulled over to the right. A black-and-white police car passed them. The red car ahead of Carmen pulled off the road. The police car stopped behind it. Its blue lights flashed.

"I'm glad I don't have to stop for *those* lights," Carmen said. "I won't complain any more about the other flashing lights."

Ms. Moss laughed. "This has been a good lesson on waiting for flashing lights. You've done a good job today, Carmen."

Story 2: Exercise

Fill in the blank with the best answer.

1. **Main Idea:** This story is about

_____

2. **Details:** Carmen had to wait in the school parking lot because

_____

3. **Sequence:** First, Carmen drove down the turnpike. Next, she

_____

4. **Cause and Effect:** Carmen saw the police car lights. Then she

_____

5. **Drawing Conclusions:** Ms. Moss told Carmen she had done a
   good job because

_____

Story 3

Mrs. Boon had been waiting for a letter from her son, Jason. Jason was working in Africa. He was teaching English in a village in the jungle. The nearest town was two hours away by car. It took letters three weeks to get to his parents.

A letter finally came. Mrs. Boon opened it. It contained a big surprise.

"Dear Mom and Dad," the letter said. "I am planning to get married. Kara Vine works in the same school. She teaches math. We want to get married in early July. I hope you can come to the wedding. It won't be an easy trip for you. I know you don't feel safe riding the subway into the city. How will you feel about a safari into Africa?

"I think you should come to Africa by airplane. Or you could come by boat, if you want to take your time. It could be a vacation.

"When you get to Africa, you'll find that there are no cabs. There are buses in the big cities. A lot of people use bicycles. A few people own their own cars. But mostly people walk.

"Once you land, you'll have to travel by jeep or truck to get to my village. Your driver will be the man who takes the mail to the city. I don't have the money to pay the fare to the city. If I did, I would come meet you."

Mrs. Boon was getting very excited. She called her husband at work. He wasn't there. He had just left and was on his way home.

Mrs. Boon got out the map of the world. Africa was a long way away.

She looked at the letter again.

"You and Dad can wear your usual clothes. Don't get too dressed up. It is very dusty here. The chief will marry us. I will wear animal skins. Kara will wear a long red skirt with animal skins for a top. This is what the tribe wears for weddings.

(continued)

"We have to pay to have a lot of food brought in by truck. This is a very poor village. There isn't much to eat besides cornmeal. After the wedding, Kara and I will travel by motorcycle to the African coast for a few days."

Mrs. Boon took a deep breath. This was going to be an adventure. She called a travel agency. She asked what it would cost for two tickets to Africa.

When she heard the price, she almost fainted. It would cost two thousand dollars for the round-trip tickets.

She thought for a moment. If Jason got married at home, they would spend almost that much. "OK," she said. "I'd like two plane tickets for July 1."

Just then, Mr. Boon walked in the door. "Plane tickets for the first of July?" he asked. "Where in the world are we going?"

"About halfway around the world," Mrs. Boon said.

She held out the letter for him to read. "Too bad we don't have a pilot in the family. Then we could fly to Africa for free. This is going to be some trip," he said.

"And some wedding," Mrs. Boon said, smiling.

❖

Survival Vocabulary Stories

Name _____

Date _____

Story 3: Exercise

Circle the letter of the best answer.

1. **Main Idea:** The best title for this story is

    (a) Jason Works in Africa

    (b) A Surprise Letter

    (c) An African Wedding

2. **Details:** Jason will wear

    (a) a red skirt

    (b) animal skins

    (c) a silk shirt

3. **Sequence:** First, Mrs. Boon called her husband. Then

    (a) she called the travel agent

    (b) she called Jason

    (c) she called her sister

4. **Cause and Effect:** Mrs. Boon decided to buy the airplane tickets because

    (a) she is rich

    (b) she wants to surprise her husband

    (c) a wedding at home would cost almost as much

5. **Drawing Conclusions:** This is going to be exciting for Mr. and Mrs. Boon because

    (a) they don't usually travel anywhere

    (b) their son is getting married

    (c) both a and b

Survival Vocabulary Stories

Story 4

Kim left her country in a boat. Her mother, father, six brothers, and her grandmother went, too. They were trying to get to a new country. There they would be safe. Many people were on board. The boat was a small one. Kim couldn't take anything with her. There was no room on the boat.

For many days, they rowed across the sea. They had very little to eat. Sometimes the waves were big. Then Kim was scared. She was afraid they would tip over. People felt seasick in the small boat. Once, in the dark, a big ship almost hit them.

One morning they saw land. Kim looked and looked. After so many days at sea, she couldn't wait to walk on land again. She wondered what her new home would be like. By noon they landed. They did not speak the language of this new land. A man finally helped them. He pointed to an old green truck. He said the driver would take them to a place where they could stay. Kim's family got into the back of the truck. There was a wooden bench for a seat. Kim had to hold two of her small brothers.

They rode over a bumpy, dusty road. They saw people on bicycles. They saw a few motorcycles. They didn't see any cars or buses.

Kim was hungry. Her brother wanted a drink of water. "It won't be long now," her mother kept saying. Long until *what*, Kim wondered.

The truck stopped outside the entrance of a refugee camp. It looked like a small city to Kim. It had rows and rows of buildings with tin roofs. People were everywhere. At least they spoke Kim's language.

After another long wait, Kim's family was given a space in a crowded building. Kim had to share a bed with her baby brother.

A woman in a brown dress came to talk to Kim's family. She gave them a map of the camp. She showed them where to go to eat. Then she looked at Kim.

(continued)

"You look like you should be in school," she said.

Kim smiled and nodded her head.

"Here is where we have our own school." The woman pointed to a place on the map. "You come tomorrow. You will learn English. Some day you may go to North America."

"I don't want to go anywhere," Kim said. She was thinking about their long boat ride.

"We'll see," the woman said.

Kim's family lived in the camp for three years. Kim studied hard. She was the first one in her family to learn English. She read books about the United States and Canada. She learned that someday her family would get tickets to fly in an airplane to North America.

Kim saw pictures of an airport. She saw pictures of a pilot in uniform. She learned how to say, "Which way is the elevator?" She learned how to say, "Where do we go to get our bags?"

From the airport they might ride in a cab or on a subway or on a train to get to their new home. She studied the maps every day. At night, she began to dream of a trip to North America.

One day, a man from Canada came to the camp. He found Kim's family. His church wanted to help Kim's family go to Canada. Kim's uncle and aunt were already there. They could help Kim's family get settled.

Kim could hardly believe her ears. It was the chance she had dreamed about. They would leave on a bus in two days. They would travel to an airport. A big airplane would take them to Ontario. Kim was so happy. This would be a trip she would never forget.

Story 4: Exercise

Fill in the blanks with the best answer.

1. **Main Idea:** What do you think is a good title for this story?

   _____

2. **Details:** How many people in Kim's family were on the boat?

   _____

3. **Details:** Why were they going to a new country?

   _____

4. **Cause and Effect:** Kim's family could go to Canada because

   _____

5. **Drawing Conclusions:** Why was Kim so happy about the trip to Canada?

   _____

6. **Activity:** Talk to someone you know who came from a different country. Ask the person about the trip. Write a few paragraphs about what you are told.

Survival Vocabulary Stories

Story 5

Fred felt like doing something daring. It was a bright summer morning. It was his day off from work.

He didn't have a car. He didn't want to spend his money on bus or train fare.

"I guess I'll ride my bicycle into town," he said to his mom. "Don't worry about me until dinnertime."

"Why? What are you going to do?" his mom asked.

"I'm not sure. I just feel like going somewhere," Fred said.

"Well, be careful," his mom said.

Fred picked up an orange and a bag of chips. He stuffed them into his backpack. He filled his water bottle. He grabbed his helmet. "Where's the map, Mom?" he yelled. His mom was on her way to catch the bus to work.

"Check in the truck. Dad had it last," she called back.

Fred put air in his bicycle tires. He fixed the seat so it was just right. Then he took off. The wind felt good on his face. He rode as fast as he could. No matter how fast he pedaled, he didn't go as fast as he wanted to. A motorcycle went zooming past him.

"I wish I had a motorcycle like that," Fred said to himself.

He rode his bicycle all the way to the river. He rode down under the railroad bridge. He sat on the river bank and ate his orange.

No other people were around. A family of ducks swam toward him. He threw them a few chips. He watched a boat coming upriver.

Now, *that's* really traveling, Fred thought. He walked along the side of the river. He wanted to get a closer look at the boat.

(continued)

Survival Vocabulary Stories

Then he walked back toward his bicycle. He sat down. He leaned back on some flat, warm rocks. He closed his eyes. Then he fell asleep.

Fred began to dream that he was taking a trip. In his dream, he was a rich man. His backpack was stuffed with money. He had a fast car and a driver to take him to the airport. His seat belt was made of gold coins. He had  more than enough money to pay the fare to travel around the world. The ticket agent smiled and said, "Yes sir," when Fred bought tickets to five different places.

On the plane, he got to sit in the cockpit next to the pilot. He had his own flight attendant. She gave him cold drinks and ice cream whenever he asked. He got to watch a movie called *Fred Goes Around the World*. His first stop was Paris. He bought a silver subway pass and rode all over Paris. The city was beautiful. He took the subway to a private hotel. He had a suite all to himself. He rode the elevator up the outside of the building.

The next day, he decided to take a train to China. He bought a railroad car. He invited all his friends to go along. The conductor said he had never seen such a wild group. Fred and his friends had a big party all the way to China. Suddenly a loud train whistle blew. Another train was coming right at their train. Just as the trains were about to crash, Fred woke up. There by the river, a train was going across the bridge. The engineer was blowing the whistle.

Fred's heart was pounding. "That was quite a trip," he said. "Whew. I think I'll stick to my bicycle."

He climbed back up the river bank. He got on his bicycle. He rode into town.

He thought he might find a friend and spend the day playing video games. He'd had enough traveling.

Survival Vocabulary Stories

Name _____

Date _____

Story 5: Exercise

Fill in the blanks with the best answer.

1. **Main Idea:** This story is about a boy who

_____

_____

2. **Details:** Fred rode under the _____and

down to the_____

3. **Sequence:** Fred filled his water bottle. Then he looked for the

_____

4. **Cause and Effect:** Fred dreamed about traveling because

_____

5. **Drawing Conclusions:** Fred decided he had enough traveling because

_____

Survival Vocabulary Stories